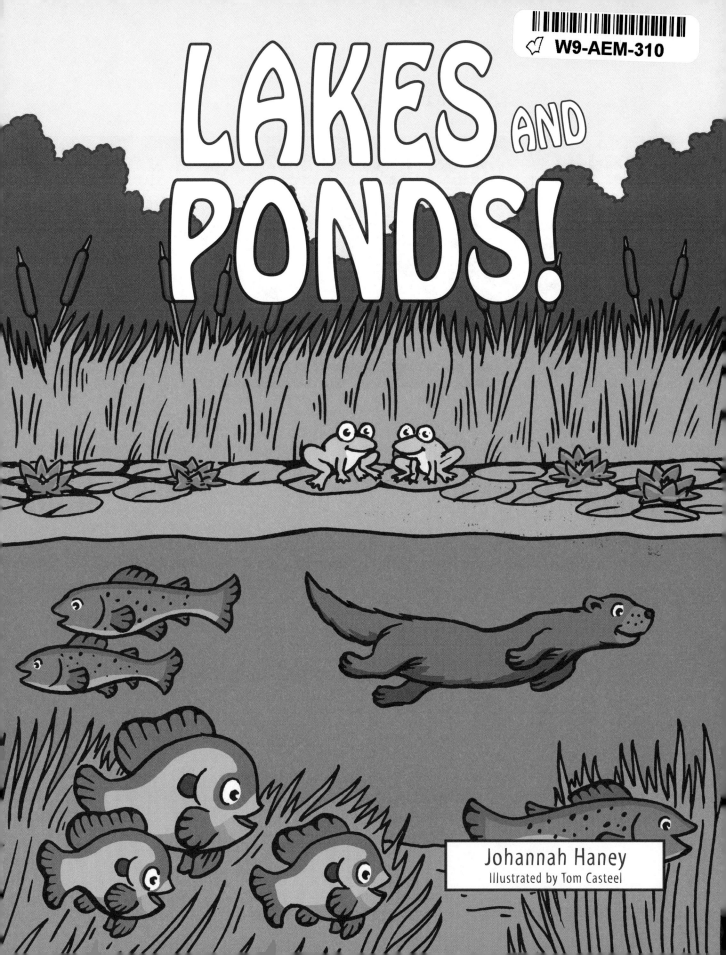

LAKES AND PONDS!

Johannah Haney
Illustrated by Tom Casteel

Titles in the **Explore Waterways** Set

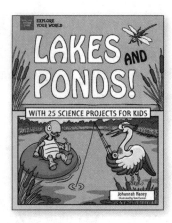
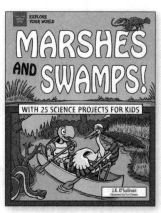
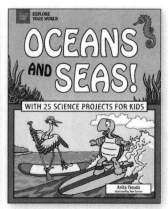
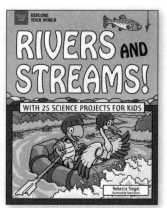

Check out more titles at www.nomadpress.net

Nomad Press
A division of Nomad Communications
10 9 8 7 6 5 4 3 2 1

This book was manufactured by Versa Press,
East Peoria, Illinois
November 2018, Job #J18-09192

ISBN Softcover: 978-1-61930-701-8
ISBN Hardcover: 978-1-61930-699-8

Educational Consultant, Marla Conn

Questions regarding the ordering of this book should be addressed to
Nomad Press
2456 Christian St.
White River Junction, VT 05001
www.nomadpress.net

CONTENTS

Interested in primary sources? Look for this icon. Use a smartphone or tablet app to scan the QR code and explore more! Photos are also primary sources because a photograph takes a picture at the moment something happens.

You can find a list of URLs on the Resources page. Try searching the internet with the Keyword Prompts to find other helpful sources.

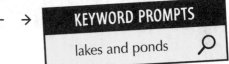

KEYWORD PROMPTS

lakes and ponds 🔍

WHAT LIVES IN LAKES AND PONDS?

Many plants and animals make their homes in lakes and ponds. Here is a glimpse of just a few—you'll meet many more in the pages of this book!

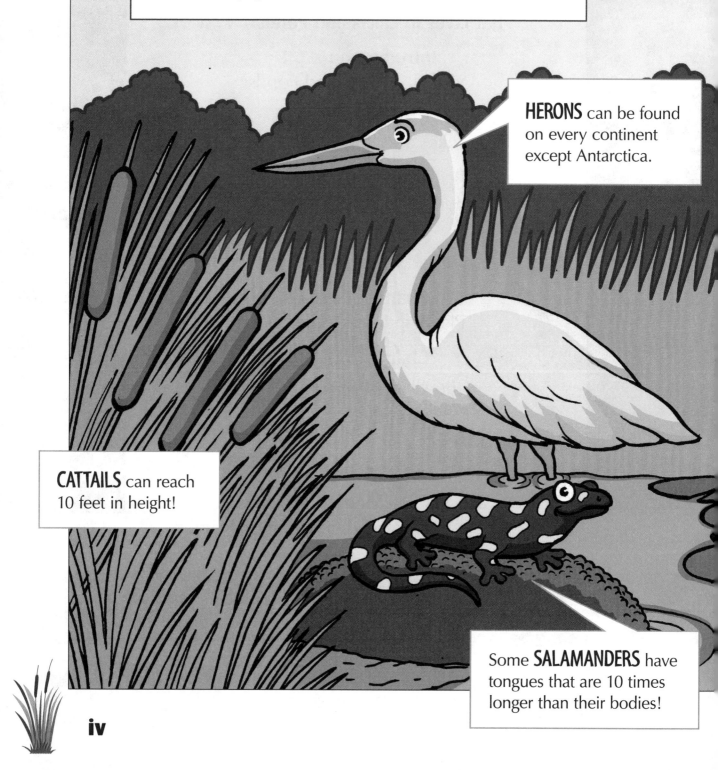

HERONS can be found on every continent except Antarctica.

CATTAILS can reach 10 feet in height!

Some **SALAMANDERS** have tongues that are 10 times longer than their bodies!

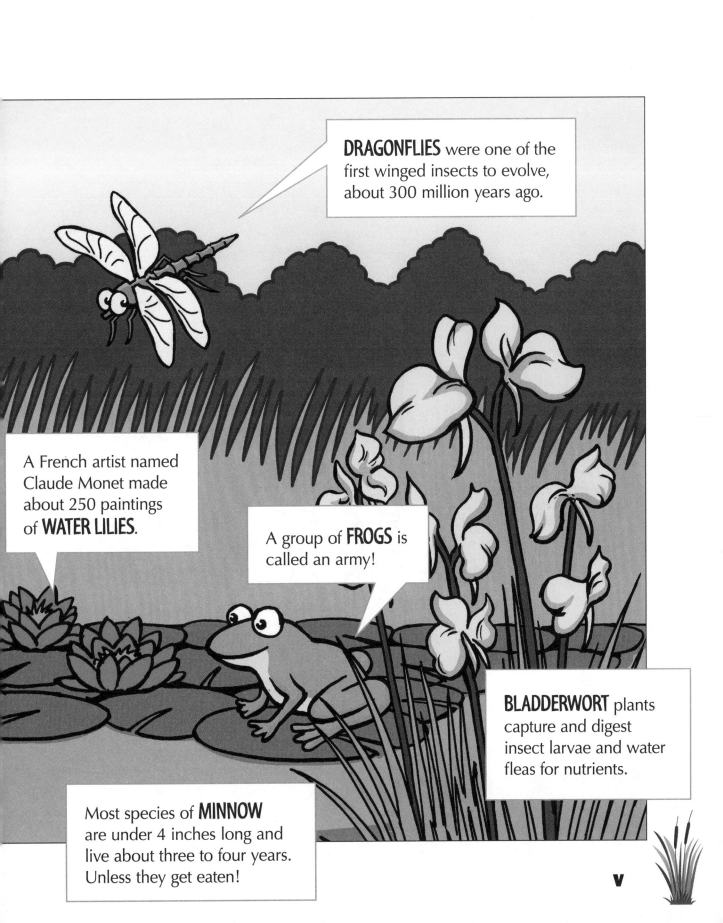

INTRODUCTION

WHAT ARE LAKES AND PONDS?

Imagine you're a turtle slipping under the surface of the fresh water of a lake. You spot schools of different types of fish swimming by. You might see the long legs of a wading bird.

You spot plenty of plants, some which are rooted in the bottom of the lakebed and others that float on the surface of the water. The lake is cool and pleasant and teeming with life!

A lake or pond is an area of slow-moving, open water surrounded by land on all sides. Lakes and ponds can be found everywhere on the earth's continents—even in deserts!

1

WORDS TO KNOW

limnologist: a person who studies inland waterways.

glaciation: the process of glaciers carving out depressions in the land, which later became lakes.

ice age: a period of time when ice covers a large part of the earth.

glacier: a huge mass of ice and snow.

saline: describes lakes and ponds that contain salt.

algae: a plant-like organism that lives in water and grows by converting energy from the sun into food.

sediment: bits of rock, sand, or dirt that have been carried to a place by water, wind, or a glacier.

What is the difference between a lake and a pond? People who study lakes and ponds are called limnologists.

They will tell you that a pond is smaller and may be shallow enough to have rooted plants growing across its entire bottom. Lakes are larger and are often deeper. While they may be full of plant life, plants with roots cannot live in the deepest depths.

HOW DO LAKES AND PONDS FORM?

Many lakes and ponds were formed by a process called glaciation. During the last ice age, between about 10,000 to 20,000 years ago, huge glaciers slid slowly across the land.

LAKE HILLIER

Lake Hillier is a saline lake on an island off the western coast of Australia. Because of a certain type of algae called *Dunaliella salina* that live in the waters, the lake appears bubblegum pink when viewed from above, and a clear pink when viewed from the ground. And it's not the only pink lake in the world! Dusty Rose Lake in British Columbia, Masazir Lake in Azerbaijan, and Laguna Colorada in Colombia are all lakes with pink colors because of algae, salt, or red sediments.

As the ice moved, it carved out deep gashes in the land, called depressions. When the glaciers melted, these depressions filled up with water, making many of the lakes and ponds we enjoy today.

The basin of a lake or pond is the hollowed-out area of the earth that fills with water. Lakes and ponds that were formed from glaciation are called glacial lakes. When you swim in a glacial lake, you are swimming where an enormous block of ice once sat!

Other lakes and ponds are caused by the movement of tectonic plates. These are the large sections of the earth's crust that fit together like puzzle pieces.

WHY SHOULDN'T YOU TELL JOKES ON A FROZEN LAKE?

It might crack up!

depression: a hole or low spot in the land.

basin: a hollow in the land into which water flows, forming a waterway.

glacial lake: a lake formed by the movement of glaciers.

tectonic plates: large sections of the earth's crust that move on top of the hot, melted layer below.

crater lake: a lake formed by a collapsed volcano.

WORDS TO KNOW

CRATER LAKES

When you think of volcanoes, you probably think of a mountain with steam and smoke escaping from the hole on top, and maybe even lava running down the side. Did you know volcanoes can turn into lakes? These are called crater lakes. One of the most famous crater lakes in the United States is Crater Lake in Oregon. Almost 8,000 years ago, Mount Mazama volcano collapsed, leaving a basin that is now filled with pure, clear water. This is the deepest lake in the United States! Learn more about Crater Lake on page 64.

WORDS TO KNOW

tectonic lake: a lake formed in cracks made by the movement of tectonic plates.

meteorite: a meteor, which is a small piece of rock from space that hits the earth's surface.

asteroid: a small, rocky object that orbits the sun.

extraterrestrial lake: a lake formed in the crater left by the impact of an asteroid or meteorite.

When tectonic plates move, the earth's crust can crack. When those cracks fill with water, a lake or pond, called a tectonic lake, is formed.

Some lakes have basins that formed from a meteorite or asteroid striking Earth. These are called extraterrestrial lakes. One extraterrestrial lake in North America is Pingualuit Crater Lake in the Nunavik region of Québec, Canada. About 1.4 million years ago, a meteorite struck the earth, burning a giant hole in the land.

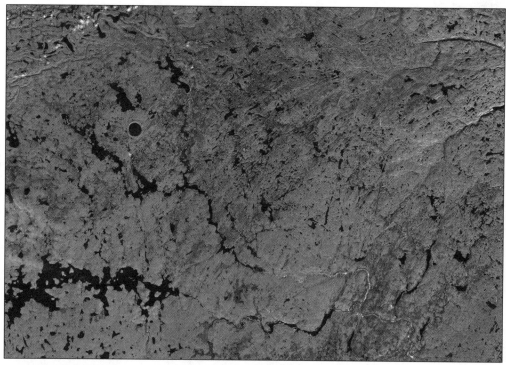

CAN YOU SEE WHERE THE EARTH CRACKED IN THIS PICTURE?   CREDIT: NASA

The crater is more than 2 miles wide and 800 feet deep. As time passed, the crater filled with water from rain and melting snow. This means Pingualuit Crater Lake has some of the clearest, purest water in the world.

WORDS TO KNOW

Inuit: the native people who live in northern Canada, parts of Greenland, and Alaska.

crater: a large, bowl-shaped hole in the ground caused by an impact.

dam: a natural or man-made barrier to flowing water.

crops: plants grown for food and other uses.

organic lake: a lake formed by animals or when vegetation or mud stops the flow of water.

vegetation: all the plant life in a particular area.

Dams are another way that lakes and ponds can form. A dam is a structure that creates a barrier to stop water from flowing. Dams are built to prevent flooding, provide a source of water for crops, and generate electricity.

Some dams are made by animals. Have you ever seen a beaver dam in a river? This collection of mud, logs, and sticks can cause water to stand still and form a lake. These are called organic lakes. Organic lakes can also be formed by a clump of vegetation that stops water from flowing.

In other instances, landslides or mudslides can create a basin into which water flows to make a lake or pond. Whenever it rains or snows, water is added.

LAKES AND PONDS!

LAYERS IN LAKES

The water in a lake is divided into three main zones: the littoral zone, the limnetic zone, and the profundal zone. The littoral zone is the shallowest area of the lake.

Sunlight can reach all the way down to the sediment bed in the littoral zone. Plenty of plants thrive here on the edges of the lake.

Next is the limnetic zone. Here, the water is so deep that plants cannot root, but free-floating plants such as phytoplankton can survive just fine.

Finally comes the profundal zone. This zone is so deep that light cannot reach it, and no plants grow here.

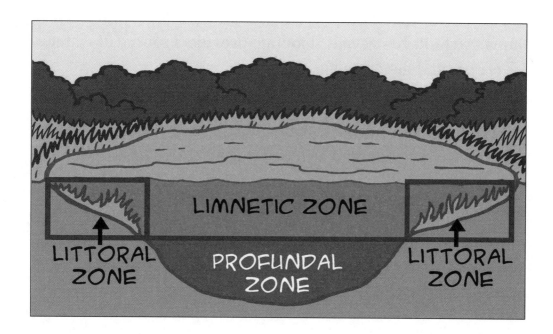

LIMNETIC ZONE

LITTORAL ZONE   PROFUNDAL ZONE   LITTORAL ZONE

DID YOU KNOW?

When there is a problem in a lake or pond that makes swimming or boating unsafe, local economies can suffer.

fisheries: places where fish are caught or raised as a business.

economy: the wealth and resources of an area or country.

WORDS ⊙ KNOW

WHY ARE LAKES AND PONDS IMPORTANT?

Lakes and ponds have been important to humans throughout time. In our hunting and gathering days, lakes were an important source of food. Hunters used spears to kill fish to eat. People also used the plant life near lakes and ponds as a source of food.

As time passed, people developed new and better tools, including different kinds of fishing nets and traps to catch more fish. When they caught more fish than they needed for themselves, fishermen sold those fish to other people.

Today, fisheries are important to the economy of places near lakes and ponds in the United States and around the world.

7

LAKES AND PONDS!

Lakes also became important when people wanted to move goods to other areas. Boats moved resources such as coal, food, and other goods across bodies of water, including the Great Lakes.

Have you ever gone swimming at a lake? Lakes and ponds can be important to an area's tourism. People visit lakes to swim, camp, and boat.

Sometimes, humans damage the lakes and ponds we depend on for food and fun. Pollution from farms and other activities can hurt lakes and ponds. That's why we all must work to keep the planet's waterways as clean as possible.

In this book, you'll learn lots more about lakes and ponds. You'll meet some of the plants and animals that live in these watery worlds and discover more about the relationship between lakes, ponds, and humans.

Along the way, you'll conduct fun science experiments to see how different lakes and ponds formed and how more might form or disappear in the future. You'll also discover ways of helping keep waterways healthy and clean. Ready? Let's go!

GOOD SCIENCE PRACTICES

Every good scientist keeps a science journal. Choose a notebook to use as your science journal. Write down your ideas, observations, and comparisons as you read this book.

For most of the projects in this book, make and use a scientific method worksheet, like the one shown here. Scientists use the scientific method to keep their experiments organized. A scientific method worksheet will help you keep track of your observations and results.

Each chapter of this book begins with a question to help guide your exploration of lakes and ponds.

Scientific Method Worksheet
Question: What problem are we trying to solve?
Research: What information is already known?
Hypothesis/Prediction: What do I think the answer will be?
Equipment: What supplies do I need?
Method: What steps will I follow?
Results: What happened and why?

? **INVESTIGATE!**

Why are lakes and ponds important to humans and animals?

Keep the question in your mind as you read the chapter. Record your thoughts, questions, and observations in your science journal. At the end of each chapter, use your science journal to think of answers to the question. Does your answer change as you read the chapter?

LAKE-TOP LIVING

SUPPLIES

* ✳ building supplies
  such as empty
  water bottles,
  lengths of pool
  noodles, and
  strips of bamboo
* ✳ packing tape
* ✳ cardboard
* ✳ large plastic
  bin or kiddie
  pool
* ✳ water

What happens when a lake grows and shrinks according to the season? How do people live and work on a lake that's always moving its shores? Residents on Tonlé Sap in Cambodia solved this problem by building a floating village. Imagine you are building a brand new floating village. What do you think would be good building materials? Use the scientific method to test different ways to make a cardboard structure float.

1 Make a plan for a floating house in your science journal. Brainstorm how you will make your house float. This is the design phase of the project. Be creative! How big do you want to make your buildings? How will you connect pieces of cardboard to build your lake-top village? What kinds of buildings will a floating village need?

2 Add water to the plastic bin. Experiment with making your floating village actually float! Before building a large structure, practice making some floating platforms and test them in water to see if they will float. Make any changes that you think will improve the design. What do you think is the best way to attach the buildings to the floating platforms?

3 Build the buildings out of cardboard and tape. Before you place the buildings on the floating platforms, make sure you are confident that the buildings won't sink! Consider the weight and shape of the buildings and how well they will be supported by the floating platforms.

PROJECT!

4 Test your floating village! Place each building and its floating platform into the tub or pool. The water level should be low. Next, start filling up the tub or pool with more water to simulate the rising lake levels of the wet season. Try to keep the buildings dry as you add more water—add it slowly and close to the surface of the water.

THINK ABOUT IT! How did your floating village turn out? If you could do something differently next time around, what would it be? Why? What challenges do you think the people living on Tonlé Sap face in their day-to-day life living on a lake?

THE RISE AND FALL OF TONLÉ SAP

Tonlé Sap is a large lake in Cambodia. During the rainy season, the lake swells to its largest size, up to 45 feet deep and about 4,000 square miles. That's almost seven times the size of Houston, Texas! But during the dry season, it shrinks to about 1,000 square miles and is just about 7 feet deep. Residents there have built a floating village. Homes rise up along with water levels and sink back down during the dry season. Tonlé Sap is a difficult place to live. Many of its residents rely on fishing to support their families, and many live in poverty. But there is also a strong community spirit that matches the magic of a floating village on a rising and falling lake.

PS You can see some of the places and people of the floating village in this video.

KEYWORD PROMPTS

Tonlé Sap video

CHAPTER 1

WHY LAKES AND PONDS ARE IMPORTANT

What do you usually reach for when you're really thirsty? Water! What do plants and crops need to grow and provide us with food? Water! How do we stay clean? You guessed it—water!

Lakes and ponds hold a lot of the planet's fresh water supply. We drink water from lakes and ponds after it's been purified. We use fresh water to keep our plants growing, which gives us the food we eat.

? INVESTIGATE!

Imagine a day without water. What kinds of activities would you need to give up? What would be different about your day?

Fresh water keeps us clean, too. We use it to brush our teeth, take showers and baths, wash our hands—everything!

THE WATER WE DRINK

Water in lakes and ponds, called surface water, is drunk by wild animals without any purification. They don't have a choice! But people shouldn't drink water straight out of lakes and ponds, just in case it makes them sick.

purification: the process of making fresh water safe for humans to drink.

surface water: water that collects in lakes, rivers, and oceans on the surface of the earth.

thermal stratification: the separation of a lake into three different zones of temperature.

epilimnion: the top layer of lake water.

metalimnion: the middle layer of lake water.

hypolimnion: the deepest layer of lake water.

WORDS TO KNOW

LAKE TEMPERATURE

Some deeper lakes experience what's called thermal stratification, meaning deeper water is colder during the summer than the water above it. The top layer of water, which is called the epilimnion, is the warmest. The middle layer, called the metalimnion, is cooler, and the deepest layer, the hypolimnion, is coldest. In the winter, the epilimnion may be colder than the layer below it if the lake is frozen. During the fall and spring, some mixing of the layers in these lakes occurs as surface water cools and sinks. We'll learn more about these layers in Chapter 5.

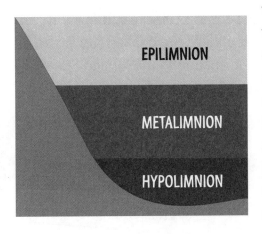

EPILIMNION

METALIMNION

HYPOLIMNION

reservoir: a man-made or natural lake used to store water for drinking and other uses.

aquifer: an underground layer of rock that has space in it that holds water.

irrigation: the process of delivering water to plants or fields where crops are planted.

erode: to gradually wear away.

stalactite: a cave formation that looks like an icicle hanging from the ceiling.

stalagmite: a cave formation that sticks up from the floor, often under a stalactite.

WORDS TO KNOW

Most of our drinking water comes from man-made reservoirs and underground lakes called aquifers. People dig deep wells to access aquifers. Now, we have water treatment plants where surface water and water from aquifers are put through the purification process to make sure the water is safe to drink.

This same fresh water is used to grow our plants. Farmers use irrigation to get water from its source to the crops.

EXPLORING UNDERGROUND LAKES

As water seeps down through the earth, it can erode softer rocks, such as limestone. The water carries these sediments down, and if the conditions are right and that water finds its way into an underground cavern, something amazing can happen. Stalactites and stalagmites form in these caverns, creating stunning displays in underground lakes and streams. Mammoth Cave in Kentucky is the largest formation in the United States, spanning 285 miles and drawing 500,000 visitors every year for cave tours.

You can take a tour of the underground cave at this website!

KEYWORD PROMPTS

NPS Mammoth Cave 🔍

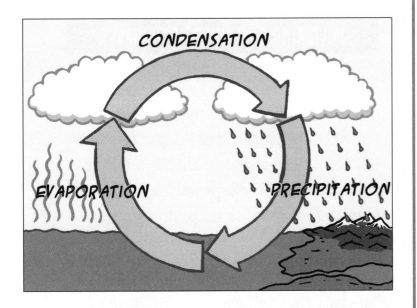

THE WATER CYCLE

If humans use so much fresh water from lakes and ponds, why doesn't it get used up? Partly because of the water cycle!

During the water cycle, water on the earth evaporates into the atmosphere, becoming invisible water vapor that rises through the air. This water vapor then cools and collects into clouds. Through the process of condensation, water vapor is turned back to liquid.

When the water droplets in the clouds get large enough, they fall back to the earth as precipitation. Even though most of the rain doesn't fall into lakes and ponds, what falls on land gets absorbed into the earth, becomes groundwater, and eventually flows into underground aquifers or into aboveground water sources. This entire process is called the water cycle.

water cycle: the continuous movement of water from the earth to the clouds and back again.

evaporation: the process of a liquid heating up and changing into a gas.

atmosphere: a blanket of gases around the earth.

water vapor: the gas form of water.

condensation: the process of a gas cooling down and changing into a liquid.

precipitation: the falling to the earth of rain, snow, or any form of water.

absorb: to soak up.

groundwater: water held underground in the soil or in cracks and crevices in rocks.

WORDS TO KNOW

hydroelectric power: electricity created by harnessing the energy of moving water.

turbine: a machine that produces energy from moving liquid or air.

nutrients: substances in food and soil that living things need to live and grow.

WORDS TO KNOW

WHAT IS THE HIGHEST COMPLIMENT YOU CAN GIVE TO A LAKE?

You are gorges!

POWERING OUR LIVES WITH WATER

Surface water from lakes does a lot more than keep us from going hungry and thirsty. Water also keeps the lights on! Electricity created through water, called hydroelectric power, is a form of energy that creates no pollution. Here's how it works.

Humans build dams on rivers. As water passes through the dam and into the river below, a turbine uses the water pressure to create electricity.

This kind of energy has drawbacks, however. Dams affect plant and animal life. They also produce more sediment in the artificial lakes they create, which can add more nutrients to the water and lead to an abnormally large bloom of algae. This happens when so much algae thrive in a body of water that it's impossible for any other life to survive there.

Since early times, humans have depended on lakes and ponds for many different things. We'll find out more about this relationship in the next chapter!

CONSIDER AND DISCUSS

It's time to consider and discuss: Imagine a day without water. What kinds of activities would you need to give up? What would be different about your day?

PROJECT!

COLD WATER SINKS

Water of different temperatures has different densities. The differences cause the water to form different layers in a lake. You can see this at work by making a lake of your own in a clear bowl!

1 Fill a glass with water and use food coloring to make the water a vivid blue color. Pour the water in an ice cube tray and put it in the freezer to make some blue ice cubes.

2 Start a scientific method worksheet. Fill the large glass bowl with lukewarm-to-warm water. Put two or three blue ice cubes gently in the water.

3 Observe what happens to the blue coloring as the ice sits in the bowl of water. What do you see? Record your observations in your science journal.

DID YOU KNOW?

Most substances are more dense as solids than as liquids, but water is different. Solid water, which is ice, is less dense than liquid water. That is why ice cubes float in water.

THINK ABOUT IT!
As soon as the ice hits the warmer water in the glass bowl, it begins to melt. The water is still quite cold, though. Which direction does the blue water move? What does that say about the density of the cold water relative to the density of the warmer water? Which one is more dense? What does this tell you about the layers of water in lakes?

WORDS TO KNOW

density: a measure of how closely packed items are.

UNDERWATER VISION

Scientists use powerful microscopes to observe underwater life forms. In this activity, make your own water scope for use in a pond or lake.

SUPPLIES

* cylindrical plastic container with a lid, such as a reusable food container
* scissors
* plastic wrap
* science journal and pencil

1 Have an adult help you cut a large hole in the bottom of the plastic container, leaving just a half-inch lip of plastic around the bottom. Do the same with the lid, again leaving about a half-inch of plastic.

2 Cover the top of your container with a piece of plastic wrap, leaving it a little loose.

3 Put the lid on over the top of the plastic wrap. This is the bottom of your scope.

4 Holding the bottom, the end with the plastic wrap down, use the scope to look into the clear shallows of a lake or pond. Be sure to keep the top of the scope above water. What do you see?

THINK ABOUT IT! Record your observations in your science journal. What do you notice about the **environment**? Did you see any animals? Plant life? You've just discovered an **ecosystem**! What changes from one part of the lake or pond to the other?

WORDS TO KNOW

environment: a natural area with animals, plants, rocks, soil, and water.

ecosystem: a community of living and nonliving things and their environment. Living things are plants, animals, and insects. Nonliving things are soil, rocks, and water.

PROJECT!

SCAVENGER HUNT!

SUPPLIES

✳ science journal and pencil

✳ magnifying glass

Time for a trip to a lake or pond! Once you're there, see how many of the items in this scavenger hunt you can find. Not every lake or pond will have everything on this list.

> **Caution:** Always have an adult with you when you are near lakes and ponds.

1 Search for things from this scavenger hunt list. Write a description of each item in your science journal.

Snail	Dragonfly nymph	Shell
White pebble	Duck	Turtle
Moss	Reed	Cattail
Pond skater	Tadpole	Adult dragonfly
Mosquito	Fish	Swan

2 Compare your findings with your friends or classmates. Can you find anything interesting that is not on this list?

THINK ABOUT IT! Did you spot any patterns when finding your items? Did a few of the items tend to be found together? Were any of the items more likely to be in warmer or colder water? What conclusions can you make about the lake environment?

PROJECT!

CONDENSATION IN A JAR

Condensation occurs when warm air meets cold air. We can use a simple setup of a jar with warm water and ice to see how condensation works.

Caution: Ask an adult help you heat the water.

1 Heat water in a pot until it is hot, but not quite boiling. Have an adult help you fill the glass jar about one-third full with the hot water.

2 Place the plate on top of the jar, completely covering the opening. Let the water in the jar sit for about 60 seconds.

3 Place ice cubes on top of the plate. What happens? Record your observations in your science journal.

THINK ABOUT IT! When you place the plate on top of the jar, you trap warmth inside. What happens to the plate on top? How does this affect the ice cubes on the plate?

TRY THIS! After the plate with ice has been on the jar for a few moments, remove the plate, quickly spray a spritz of hair spray in the jar, and replace the plate with ice. What happens now?

20

PROJECT!

WATER CYCLE IN THE WINDOW

The water cycle is the process of water evaporating, condensing in clouds, and falling back to Earth in the form of precipitation. Let's create our own microclimate **and make it rain!**

1 Using your marker, draw a picture of a lake at the bottom of the plastic bag. Draw a cloud toward the top of the bag. Fill in details of the water cycle. Show where water vapor rises and where rain falls.

2 Put about half a cup of water inside the plastic bag to fill the bottom of the bag. Add blue food coloring. You've made a pond.

3 Tape your water cycle microclimate to a window that gets sun. Make sure to use lots of tape to support the weight of the water! What do you think is going to happen to the water in the bottom of the plastic bag? Why? Start a scientific method worksheet in your science journal and record your predictions.

4 During the next several days, observe what happens to the water in your microclimate. In your science journal, note how much sun the microclimate gets.

THINK ABOUT IT! Were the days sunny? Partly cloudy? How might that affect your results? Do you ever notice drops of water clinging to the side of the bag? What does that represent? How might your results be different if you had placed your microclimate in a different spot?

WORDS TO KNOW

microclimate: the climate of a very small area.

21

PROJECT!

BUILD A WATER FILTER

Certain types of rock are best for purifying groundwater in aquifers. You can make your own version of this natural type of water filter.

1 Cut off the bottom of an empty 2-liter bottle. Recycle the bottom and the lid.

2 Tip the bottle upside down and rest the top of the bottle inside the vase.

3 Fill the bottle with a 2-inch layer of cotton balls. Add a layer of about an inch of activated charcoal.

4 Layer 2 to 3 inches of gravel or pebbles on top of the charcoal. Add 4 inches of sand to the top.

5 In a separate cup, mix dirt with water. Pour the dirty water over the sand. What happens? Record your observations in your science journal.

SUPPLIES

* ❋ empty 2-liter bottle
* ❋ scissors or a knife
* ❋ vase
* ❋ cotton balls
* ❋ activated charcoal from a drugstore
* ❋ gravel or small pebbles
* ❋ sand
* ❋ cup
* ❋ dirt
* ❋ water
* ❋ science journal and pencil

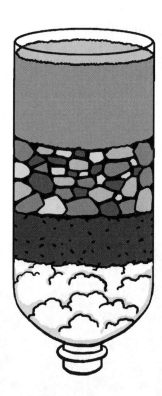

scarcity: too little of something.

WORDS TO KNOW

THE WHOLE WORLD NEEDS FRESH WATER

According to the United Nations, about one-fifth of the world's population lives in an area of water **scarcity**. That means that about 1.2 billion people don't have easy access to clean drinking water. Even though there is enough water in the world for all 7 billion people, it is not available to everyone in the same amounts because water is not distributed evenly around the world. There are 43 countries that have water shortages right now, and another 500 million people are approaching water scarcity. What can you do to help? Start by conserving water whenever you can. Turn off the water when brushing your teeth and take shorter showers.

THINK ABOUT IT! Watch as the water filters through all the different layers. What is happening to the dirt in the water you poured through your homemade filter? In your science journal, describe how this process is like the natural process of groundwater purification in aquifers.

TRY THIS! Can you think of any additional materials you could add to the top layer to make the filter even more successful? What else can you use to purify your water?

PROJECT!

VISUALIZING STRATIFICATION

SUPPLIES

✳ large, clear bowl
✳ 2 cups blueberries
✳ 1 cup raspberries
✳ ½ cup cherries
✳ spoon

Water in deeper ponds and lakes can be different temperatures at different depths. Using the vocabulary you have learned, recreate the layers of thermal stratification in a lake. Feel free to substitute different fruits or even different foods!

1 Place 2 cups of blueberries in the bottom of the bowl. On top of the blueberries, pour 1 cup of raspberries. On top of the raspberries, pour ½ cup of cherries. Which layer do you think represents the epilimnion? Which represents the metalimnion? Which represents the hypolimnion?

2 Now, take the spoon and mix up all the fruits in your bowl. What action does this simulate?

DID YOU KNOW?

About 97 percent of the water on Earth is salt water and is in the oceans. Two percent is frozen in ice. The other 1 percent is found in lakes, ponds, rivers, groundwater, and clouds—this is where all our fresh water comes from!

THINK ABOUT IT!

Imagine the bowl is a lake and the different fruits represent different water temperatures. Colder water is more dense and it sinks. During the summer, the top layer of water is warmed by the sun. As temperatures drop during the fall, cooling the surface water, this colder water sinks, mixing the water in the lake or pond. Wind can also contribute to mixing the layers.

CHAPTER 2

HUMANS, LAKES, AND PONDS

Have you ever gone for a swim in a pond? Taken a boat ride across a lake? You're one example of a human interacting with nature. All over the world, humans interact with lakes and ponds millions of times every single day.

In the last chapter, we learned about lakes and ponds as sources of drinking water, food, and electricity. In this chapter, we'll explore other ways humans use lakes and ponds.

? INVESTIGATE!

How does human activity affect lakes and ponds?

How might early humans have used lakes and ponds that's different from how we use them now? How has human history been affected by the waterways of the world?

LAKE, HO!

Throughout history, humans have left their homes to explore other lands. Because people can carry only a limited amount of supplies with them, many travelers planned their routes and destinations with the hope that they'd find food and clean water on the journey. This meant they followed the water.

Many important events and discoveries in North America have taken place around lakes and ponds. For example, in the 1600s, French explorers became the first Europeans to see the Great Lakes.

WHY DOES LAKE SUPERIOR HAVE SUCH HIGH SELF-ESTEEM?

Not only is it superior, it is also Great!

The discovery laid the groundwork for Europeans to settle in what's now the Midwest United States. It led to the founding of major cities such as Chicago, Illinois; Milwaukee, Wisconsin; Detroit, Michigan; and Cleveland, Ohio.

Lake Tahoe, on the border of what is now California and Nevada, was an important source of fish for the Washoe tribe of Native Americans. In 1844, the explorer John Charles Frémont (1813–1890) encountered what is now known as Lake Tahoe. Just 14 years later, a valuable natural resource was found about 25 miles away. Silver mining soon began in what was called the Comstock Lode.

natural resource: something found in nature that is useful to humans, such as water to drink, trees to burn and build with, and fish to eat.

mining: taking minerals from the ground, such as silver or iron ore.

WORDS TO KNOW

SHIPWRECK! A GREAT LAKES MYSTERY

In the seventeenth century, a French ship named *Le Griffon* went missing in Lake Michigan. This ship was built by the famous French explorer, René-Robert Cavelier de la Salle (1643–1687). Its maiden voyage began on August 7, 1679, and wound through Lakes Erie, Huron, and Michigan. On its way back from a trading expedition, the ship disappeared. No one knows for sure what happened to the ship. Some people think it was captured and burned, while others believe that the shipwreck must be somewhere on the bed of Lake Michigan. Shipwreck hunters continue to search for remains of the ship today, just one of many hundreds of shipwrecks in the Great Lakes.

WORDS TO KNOW

industry: a business that provides a product or service.

solar system: the collection of eight planets, moons, and other celestial bodies that orbit the sun.

celestial body: a star, planet, moon, or other object in space.

hydrocarbon: a chemical compound that contains hydrogen and carbon. Oil and natural gas are hydrocarbons.

Lake Tahoe was used to transport goods for the logging and mining industry. As people moved into the Lake Tahoe area to become part of these new industries, the lake was also used as a place for people to relax. Today, it is a major tourist destination with lots of sports activities, such as skiing, scuba diving, and water skiing.

MODERN EXPLORATION OF LAKES

Lake exploration is still happening! Russian scientists are currently studying Lake Vostok in Antarctica.

LAKES IN OUTER SPACE

Earth is the only planet in our solar system that has bodies of water. However, other celestial bodies have lakes! NASA recently discovered that Titan, one of the moons that orbits around Saturn, has seas and lakes composed of

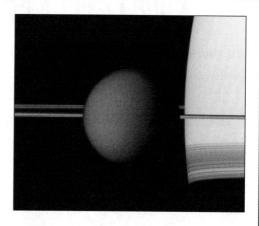

hydrocarbons and water ice. What's more, they're connected by underground aquifers, just as we have on Earth. Because of the data collected by NASA's *Cassini* spacecraft in 2017, we now know that Titan is the most Earth-like of any known world in the universe.

Lake Vostok is a subglacial lake, which means it lies underneath a massive glacier. Scientists have worked for years in frigid temperatures to drill through more than 2 miles of ice so they could study the fresh water trapped underneath.

Antarctica has more than 350 subglacial lakes. They stay in liquid form instead of freezing because they're under pressure from the glacier above and warmed by the heat of the earth from below.

An American team is currently exploring Lake Whillans in Antarctica and the British Antarctic Survey is exploring Lake Ellsworth. Because these ecosystems are totally undisturbed, they could hold new life forms that humans haven't discovered yet. Astrobiologists—scientists who study life on other planets—are interested in the life in subglacial lakes because those icy conditions are similar to those on some moons in the solar system.

WORDS TO KNOW

subglacial lake: a freshwater lake underneath a glacier.

astrobiologist: a scientist who studies life in space.

DID YOU KNOW?

When explorers with the Loch Ness Project were searching for the legendary Loch Ness Monster in Scotland in 2016, they found something at the bottom of the lake: Nessie herself! Except what they really found was a massive movie prop that sunk during production of the 1970 movie *The Private Life of Sherlock Holmes*.

PS

Travel along with the Undersea Voyager Project as it explores Fallen Leaf Lake, south of Lake Tahoe in California.

KEYWORD PROMPTS

California Diver Undersea Fallen Leaf video

LAKES AND PONDS!

Researchers with the Undersea Voyager Project explored Lake Tahoe in 2016 and found trees that were more than 2,000 years old, shipwrecks from a century ago, and what they believe is a previously undiscovered life form. Whiskeytown Lake in California has a sunken mining town from the Gold Rush that was flooded after a dam was built in the 1960s. Lake exploration is still important in today's world.

LAKE INDUSTRY

Did you know that whole industries are based on lakes? Aquaculture, which is the farming

of fish and other organisms that live in the water, takes place both in the oceans and in freshwater lakes.

Fish and shellfish farming provides food to humans and animals. Aquaculture also helps prevent overfishing, which is harmful to wild species. Lake Victoria, the largest freshwater lake in Africa, supports 35 million people by providing food, water, and jobs. But because the lake has been badly overfished in the last few decades, the ecosystem of the lake is in peril.

There are currently severe restrictions on fishing in Lake Victoria. People hope these restrictions will help restore fish populations, bring the lake's ecosystem back into balance, and make it healthy again.

Larger lakes are rich in natural resources, and companies mine lakebeds to harvest and sell these resources and make money. In the last few years, billions of barrels of oil have been discovered under the lakes of the East Africa Rift System in Kenya and Ethiopia. Drilling for that oil has added millions of dollars to the economies of those countries and has provided the world with a new source of oil, which powers cars and heats homes.

DID YOU KNOW?

The United States is the fifth largest producer of fish in the world, behind China, India, Indonesia, and Peru. The country's largest fishery is on Lake Erie, which catches mostly walleye and yellow perch.

LAKE VICTORIA IN UGANDA

outlet: a river or stream connected to a lake or other body of water that allows water to flow out.

WORDS ᴛᴏ KNOW

Drilling for oil has its drawbacks. Lake Kivu, in western Africa, is being explored for its rich oil reserves. Because the lake is so deep, the water at the bottom is very dense. The lowest layer, the hypolimnion, can't release gases into the air.

As a result of the oil drilling, there is a large gas buildup at the bottom of the lake. If it's disturbed, it could cause the lake to explode! We'll explore more about how lakes are changing because of people in Chapter 6.

Humans aren't the only ones with a strong connection to lakes and ponds. In the next chapter, we'll see how other creatures live in and use these environments.

CONSIDER AND DISCUSS

It's time to consider and discuss: How does human activity affect lakes and ponds?

GET TO KNOW: THE GREAT SALT LAKE

Most salt water is in the oceans—but not all of it! Lakes can have salt water, too. Aside from the Great Lakes, the largest lake in the United States is the Great Salt Lake in Utah. It's salty because it has no river or other water outlet. The lake's only method of losing water is by evaporation, so it accumulates more salt than most other lakes. It's even saltier than the ocean! Ever since a railroad line was built across the lake in the early 1900s, something curious has happened—the lake has become two different colors! Because the salinity is different on each side of the railroad line, different algae grows in the two halves, making one half very bright blue and the other half reddish brown.

PROJECT!

SINK OR SWIM

Salty water, like that in the Great Salt Lake in Utah, provides more buoyancy **than fresh water. Things float more easily in salty water. Let's experiment with saline water vs. fresh water. Start a scientific method worksheet in your science journal to organize your experiment.**

1 Measure 1½ cups water into each of the two drinking glasses. Add the salt to one of the glasses. Stir, stir, stir! It will take a few minutes of stirring before the salt dissolves.

2 Very carefully lower an egg into each glass. You'll need to do it gently so the egg does not crack or break.

3 What happens to each egg? Why? Record your results by writing or drawing a picture in your science journal.

TRY THIS! The amount of salt in water affects its buoyancy. Once you've recorded your results, remove the egg from the saline water. Pour out one-half cup of saline water and add one-half cup of tap water back into the glass. Try placing the egg back in the solution. What happens? Take another one-half cup of water out and replace it with one-half cup of tap water. At what point will the egg stop floating?

WORDS TO KNOW

buoyancy: the ability to float.

33

CHAPTER 3

ANIMALS IN LAKES AND PONDS

Humans are not the only creatures that enjoy the bodies of water on our Earth. All kinds of animals live on, in, and around lakes and ponds!

Different lakes provide different habitats for the animals that live there. For example, some fish species prefer salt water and can live only in lakes where the salt content is much higher than in most lakes. Some creatures prefer warm water and some prefer cold.

? INVESTIGATE!

What are some ways that humans rely on the animals that live in ponds and lakes?

WELCOME TO THE ECOSYSTEM

Each pond or lake is its own unique ecosystem. Think of an ecosystem as a community of plants and animals, each with its own role to play, that live side by side and interact. An ecosystem also includes non-living things such as water, air, and soil.

Any change to one part of the ecosystem can affect the others. For example, if one kind of animal dies off, the animals that eat that animal might die off, too.

habitat: the natural area where a plant or animal lives.

Western Hemisphere: the half of the earth that contains North and South America.

crustacean: a type of animal, such as a crab or lobster, that lives mainly in water. It has several pairs of legs and its body is made up of sections covered in a hard outer shell.

aquatic: living or growing in water.

gills: filter-like structures that let an organism get oxygen out of the water to breathe.

WORDS TO KNOW

SALTY SHRIMP IN A SALTY LAKE!

The Great Salt Lake in Utah is the largest saltwater lake in the Western Hemisphere. The brine shrimp is perfectly suited to live in its salty waters. Brine shrimp are tiny crustaceans that were once widely sold under the name *sea monkey*. These aquatic creatures breathe through gills on their feet!

LAKES AND PONDS!

food chain: a community of plants and animals, where each is eaten by another higher up in the chain.

food web: a network of connected food chains that shows the complex set of feeding relationships between plants and animals.

phytoplankton: tiny, free-floating plants that live in both fresh water and salt water.

zooplankton: tiny animals that float freely in salt water and fresh water.

vertebrate: an animal with a backbone.

invertebrate: an animal without a backbone.

WORDS TO KNOW

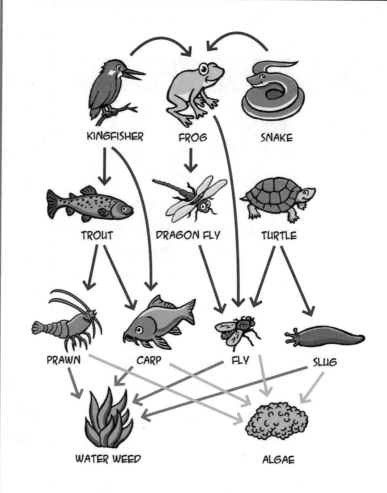

Many different food chains and food webs exist within each ecosystem. Most lake food webs begin with phytoplankton that grow on the top layer of the lake where there is plenty of sunlight. Tiny creatures called zooplankton eat phytoplankton. Small fish eat the zooplankton. Larger fish eat the smaller fish. Then birds eat the larger fish. Each life form acts as a link in the chain that provides food for the next life form. Food webs keep the lake community in balance.

Each pond or lake may have hundreds or even thousands of different organisms living within or around it. These include both vertebrates and invertebrates.

FISH

About 10,000 different species of fish live in fresh water. Because of their keen senses and swimming agility, fish are often the top predator in lakes and ponds. However, these cold-blooded creatures also become prey for other animals—especially land animals such as bears and birds.

DID YOU KNOW?

Fish are cold-blooded, which means they can't regulate their own body heat. Fish take on the temperature of their environment.

predator: an animal that hunts other animals for food.

cold-blooded: animals that have a body temperature that varies with the surrounding temperature, such as fish and snakes.

prey: an animal that is killed by another for food.

carbon dioxide: a colorless, odorless gas. It forms when animals breathe and when plants and other living matter die and rot.

WORDS ⊕ KNOW

Some fish eat by straining plankton through their gills. Fish also use gills to get the oxygen they need from the water. They take in a big mouthful of water that includes plankton, and force the water out over their gills, where the oxygen from the water gets absorbed and carbon dioxide gets rejected as waste. The plankton

WATER FLOW

GILLS

OXYGEN

CARBON DIOXIDE

are trapped in the fish! Many fish eat invertebrates such as insects or even other fish.

37

AMPHIBIANS

Toads, frogs, newts, and salamanders are some of the most popular amphibians in lakes and ponds. Like fish, amphibians are cold-blooded, but unlike fish, amphibians live on land after developing in the water. As adults, they breathe through their damp skin and must stay near water to keep it moist.

The larvae of most amphibians have gills and live underwater like fish. However, when they become adults, they grow lungs to breathe and legs to walk on land.

LIFE CYCLE OF A FROG

The life cycle of a frog is an example of metamorphosis. A mother frog lays eggs in the pond. Tadpoles emerge that look like small fish, with long tails and no legs. They breathe through gills and stay underwater all the time. Then, they begin to grow legs and lungs. Eventually, they lose their tails and their gills. They hop onto dry land as adult frogs, and begin the cycle all over again by laying eggs in the water.

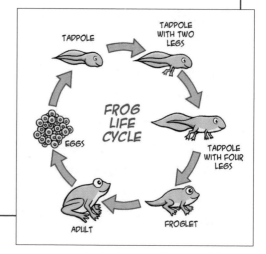

FROG LIFE CYCLE

TADPOLE

TADPOLE WITH TWO LEGS

TADPOLE WITH FOUR LEGS

FROGLET

ADULT

EGGS

REPTILES

Reptiles are often at the top of the food web because of their size and hunting abilities. Have you ever seen turtles, snakes, alligators, or crocodiles? These are all reptiles! Reptiles are cold-blooded animals with scales or hard plates. Reptiles lay eggs in leathery shells on land.

With the exception of turtles, all reptiles have teeth. The biggest fangs can be found on alligators and crocodiles. They live in both fresh water and brackish water and can be dangerous to humans. By contrast, most snakes that live in or around water are harmless to humans.

BIRDS

Birds are warm-blooded creatures whose bodies are covered in feathers. They feast on food supplies found in lakes and ponds, including plants, fish, crustaceans, insects, and other animals, and make their nests along the shore. Shorebirds such as herons are easy to spot because of their long, thin legs. Waterfowl such as swans, geese, and ducks have webbed feet for swimming.

reptile: a cold-blooded animal such as a snake, lizard, alligator, or turtle, that has a spine, lays eggs, has scales or horny places, and breathes air.

brackish: water that contains both salt water and fresh water.

evolve: to gradually develop through time.

warm-blooded: animals that can keep themselves warm with their own body heat, such as humans, birds, and bears.

WORDS TO KNOW

DID YOU KNOW?

Freshwater turtles are among the oldest reptiles on Earth! Most species of turtle have not evolved much during the course of 200 million years.

Ducks are attracted to ponds not just for food but because of the safe haven they provide from predators on land. Large birds of prey such as ospreys and eagles swoop down from the air to catch fish.

MAMMALS

Lots of mammals live near ponds and lakes and depend on them for food and water. Mammals are warm-blooded creatures that do not lay eggs, and their skin is usually covered in hair.

Moose, deer, raccoons, foxes, wolves, bats, and bears fish, drink, hunt, swim, or scavenge in the waters or along the banks of lakes and ponds.

AN OSPREY CATCHING A FISH!   CREDIT: TONY ALTER (CC BY 2.0)

FEEDING THE DUCKS

Many people enjoy feeding ducks near the shores of lakes and ponds. While people often bring bread, it's not healthy for these waddlers. Bread doesn't contain the nutrients ducks need to be healthy. Even more, rotting bread can disrupt the ecosystem of their waters, causing harmful algae to grow that can hurt fish and make ducks sick. If you want to feed ducks, leave the loaf at home and bring lettuce, peas, or sliced seedless grapes.

Otters are the most aquatic of all these mammals. They have webbed feet and nostrils that close underwater. Their tails help them swim fast and catch fish. There is another mammal that enjoys swimming in lakes and ponds: humans!

INVERTEBRATES

Insects, crustaceans, mollusks, and microscopic creatures such as zooplankton are all cold-blooded invertebrates. These invertebrates are crucial to the life of a pond. For example, worms act as decomposers that break down the dead plants and animals that settle to the bottom of the lake. Without worms, lakes would have a lot more rotting material in them.

DID YOU KNOW?

Otters are known for being playful. They even construct slides on the banks for fun and to help them enter the water.

Invertebrates provide food for other animals in the food web. For example, insects are eaten by fish, frogs, birds, and other animals. Some insects are fully aquatic, such as the water

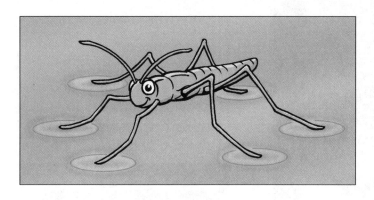

beetle, while others, such as water striders, live on and around the water.

Crustaceans are also important. Most crustaceans live underwater throughout their life cycle. Shrimp and crayfish are two examples. Mollusks are another common aquatic animal. These are soft animals that usually live inside shells—think of snails, clams, and mussels.

At the very bottom of the food web are the tiniest animals that live in lakes and ponds. These are the zooplankton that allow the rest of the pond life to flourish. Invisible to the human eye, they nevertheless have a very important role to play!

In the next chapter, we'll look at some of the plants that thrive in ponds and lakes!

DID YOU KNOW?

Ninety-seven percent of all animals in the animal kingdom are invertebrates.

? CONSIDER AND DISCUSS

It's time to consider and discuss: What are some ways that humans rely on the animals that live in ponds and lakes?

PROJECT!

HOW DO FISH BREATHE?

Gills are specialized organs that allow animals to breathe underwater. How do they work? In this activity, the water represents pond water and the dirt is a visible representation of the oxygen that is normally dissolved and invisible in water. The coffee filter acts like a fish's gills.

1 Place the coffee filter over the empty cup and secure it with a rubber band.

2 Stir the dirt into the cup of water. Pour the dirt and water mixture through the filter.

3 What is left on the filter? And below it in the cup? Record your observations in your science journal.

HOW DID THE FROG BURN ITS TONGUE?

It tried to eat a firefly!

THINK ABOUT IT! A fish gulps water with its mouth. The water then moves through the gills, which pull oxygen from the water and release carbon dioxide. The oxygen moves through the fish, while the water and carbon dioxide pass out of its body. In this activity, the oxygen (dirt) was caught by the gills (filter) and the water containing carbon dioxide passed out of them (into the cup).

PROJECT!

DRY AS A DUCK

Did you ever wonder why ducks don't get soaking wet in water? Let's find out! Start a scientific method worksheet in your science journal and make a hypothesis. What do you think will happen when you dip each card in the water?

SUPPLIES

- ✳ 2 pieces of card stock
- ✳ cooking oil
- ✳ science journal and pencil
- ✳ 2 containers of water

1 Cover one piece of card stock completely with oil, leaving the other piece as is.

2 Dip each piece of card stock in its own container of water and then remove it. What happens? Record your observations.

TRY THIS! Ducks spend most of their lives in water, but they stay dry and warm thanks to a layer of oil on their feathers. What would happen if you tried using different types of oily products on card stock? Is there one that might work as well as a duck's natural oil?

GOOD OIL VS. BAD OIL

Ducks have their own natural layer of oil, but not all oil is good for them! When humans spill oil, ducks and other aquatic animals get it on them. The oil hurts their ability to float and their natural feather insulation. When birds preen their feathers to try to get the oil off, they are poisoned. Oil spills affect food supplies and cover nests and eggs. That's why it's so important to protect our environment.

44

PROJECT!

FUN WITH FOOD CHAINS AND FOOD WEBS

SUPPLIES

* 6 Styrofoam cups that stack
* markers

Every living thing needs nutrients to live, grow, and thrive. Most types of living things get their nutrients from eating other living things. Food webs show where different life forms get their food.

1 Identify a pond food chain that contains six life forms. For example: phytoplankton, zooplankton, crustacean, amphibian, predator fish, human.

2 Turn your first cup upside down and use your marker to write the name of the first life form on the brim. Next to that label, draw a picture of the life form on the side of the cup. Repeat this with each of your cups.

3 After you finish labeling and drawing on each of your cups, stack them upside down, starting with the life form at the bottom of the food chain and working your way to the top. Now you have a visible food chain!

TRY THIS! Could this food chain be expanded into a food web that shows more relationships between life forms? Give it a try. How many chains can you connect into one larger web? What does this show you about the **interconnectivity** of life on Earth?

WORDS TO KNOW

interconnectivity: the state of being connected together.

45

POPULATION SAMPLING

Scientists sometimes learn about the number of animals living in a certain environment by counting the number that they see in a small area and then using math to make predictions about a larger area.

SUPPLIES

* a piece of construction paper
* pencil
* ruler
* ¼ cup dried beans

1 Using your pencil and ruler, draw two lines to divide your paper into four equal sections. Scatter the beans over your paper, making sure some land in each section.

2 Randomly choose one section of your paper and count the beans in it. Record the total number. Do the same for another section.

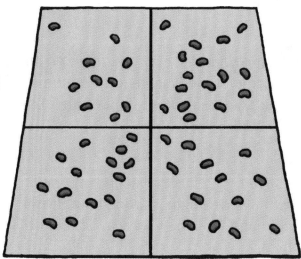

3 Find the average number of beans by adding the totals together and dividing by two.

4 Now that you have your average, take that number and multiply by four. This will give you an estimate of the total number of beans on the paper.

5 Count the actual beans on your paper. How close was the estimate in step 4 to the actual number you counted?

WORDS TO KNOW

estimate: to make a close guess.

PROJECT!

THINK ABOUT IT!
In this activity, beans represent individual animals, such as frogs or pike fish in a lake, and the paper represents the lake environment. The process is similar to population sampling, which gives an estimate (though not an exact count) of the animals in a given area. Population sampling can be useful since it's very difficult to count all the animals in the wild!

THE GREAT BACKYARD BIRD COUNT

Did you know you can be a part of the world's biggest bird count? Every February, more than 160,000 people all over the world participate in the Great Backyard Bird Count. They observe nature around them and count the number of different species of birds they see. During the last 20 years, the bird count has taken place in more than 1,000 countries and has counted more than 6,000 species of birds! To participate, register at GBBC.BirdCount.org.

 Want to be a citizen scientist? You can help count penguins with the Zooniverse website! This program uses volunteers who count animals they see in pictures, so scientists know how many penguins there are in certain places.

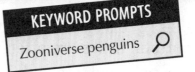

KEYWORD PROMPTS

Zooniverse penguins 🔍

CHAPTER 4

PLANTS IN LAKES AND PONDS

Ponds and lakes are home to a vast number of different species of plants. The kinds of plants found in a lake depend on different things, such as the part of the world the lake is located, the temperature of the water, whether the water is salt or fresh, and the size of the lake or pond.

In fact, plant life can be one factor that defines whether a body of water is a lake or a pond! Many ponds are shallow enough that they can support rooted plants all the way across the bottom. Lakes are often too deep for that. They may be able to support plants with roots only in the shallow water at the shore.

Let's take a closer look at the different forms of plant life in lakes and ponds.

WHAT ARE PLANTS GOOD FOR?

Without plants, there would be no life at all in lakes and ponds. Remember the food web you learned about in Chapter 3? Plants form the foundation of all life, everywhere.

One way plants support life is by oxygenating the water. Plants add oxygen to both the water and the air through the process of photosynthesis.

Plants take in sunlight and use the energy to convert carbon dioxide and water into food. This process creates oxygen, which the plants release into the water and the air since they can't use it. That makes plants incredibly important to Earth's atmosphere. They absorb the carbon dioxide that we can't breathe and add the oxygen that we need.

WORDS TO KNOW

oxygenate: to supply with oxygen.

photosynthesis: the process plants use to turn sunlight, carbon dioxide, and water into food.

? INVESTIGATE!

What type of plants are more important in a lake or pond—small plants that you need a microscope to see or big, leafy plants?

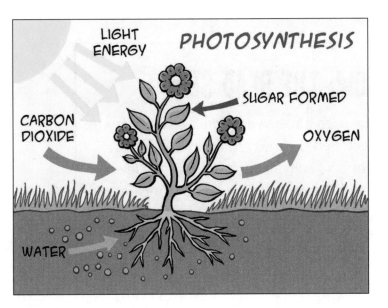

LIGHT ENERGY
PHOTOSYNTHESIS
CARBON DIOXIDE
SUGAR FORMED
OXYGEN
WATER

winterkill: when plants and fish die in frozen lakes due to reduced oxygen levels.

adapt: to make changes to better survive in an environment.

hibernate: to spend a period of time in an inactive state in order to survive harsh conditions.

bacteria: microorganisms that live in animals, plants, soil, and water. Some bacteria are helpful and some are harmful.

fungi: organisms without leaves or flowers that grow on other plants or decaying material. Singular is fungus.

WORDS TO KNOW

In lakes and ponds, plants add the oxygen to the water that fish, amphibians, reptiles, and insects need to breathe. In the winter, when many lakes ice over, ice and snow blocks sunlight from reaching the plants. The rate of photosynthesis drops, as does the oxygen level in the water.

This can cause some fish to die in a phenomenon called winterkill. Some aquatic animals have adapted to hibernate during cold winter weather. Hibernation slows down their body systems, so they require less oxygen to survive.

WHERE DO ZOMBIES LIKE TO GO SWIMMING?

The Dead Sea!

GET TO KNOW: THE DEAD SEA

The Dead Sea isn't really a sea. It's a massive saline lake in Jordan, Israel, and Palestine. The Dead Sea is almost 10 times saltier than the ocean! Because the water is so salty, it can't support any life forms bigger than bacteria and fungi, so there are no plants in its waters. And, because of its high concentration of salt, people can't swim under the water even if they try—the water pushes them right back to the surface!

cyanobacteria: a type of aquatic bacteria that produces oxygen through photosynthesis.

WORDS TO KNOW

In addition to providing oxygen, plants provide homes for lake creatures. Plants along lakeshores tend to have sturdy roots and can withstand being shoved around by waves. These plants provide habitats for many animals.

Muskrats build homes out of cattails, which are tall with long, brown tops that look like cats' tails. Bulrush, which is a tall, reedy plant that grows in shallow water, provides food and nesting areas for animals, birds, reptiles, and insects. These plants are also good for birds to nest in.

DID YOU KNOW?

The word *phytoplankton* comes from the Greek words for "wandering plants." Algae and cyanobacteria are both phytoplankton. They work hard at photosynthesis and provide much of the oxygen needed in a lake or pond.

Other plants in lakes and ponds serve another important function: food! Fish, amphibians, and many animals eat plants that grow in lakes, from very tiny algae to plants that humans can eat, too, such as wild rice, watercress, wasabi, water pepper, and water spinach.

HARMFUL PLANT LIFE

Believe it or not, sometimes plants and animals can be harmful when they're introduced into environments where they don't normally live. Non-native organisms can take over an ecosystem and push out native species.

THE IMPORTANCE OF ALGAE

We often hear bad things about algae, such as warnings of red tide and other abnormal algal blooms. Red tide is an algal bloom that can be harmful to wildlife and humans. But algae deserve more good press than bad! Through photosynthesis, algae produce 50 percent of all oxygen on the earth, which means algae give us every other breath we take. Algae are also responsible for all the crude oil and natural gas that we consume. Millions of years ago, dead plants formed coal during long periods of time, but it is algae that produced our other fossil fuels. And since algae form the base of the food web in the ocean, this phytoplankton supports all animal life in the oceans.

When this happens, an invasive species can grow or spread rapidly. This can throw off the ecosystem of any habitat, including those of lakes and ponds. In the animal world, the zebra mussel has damaged lakes and ponds. It filters out algae that native mussels need for food.

In the plant world, an example of an invasive species is purple loosestrife, which was brought to America by European immigrants in the nineteenth century because of its beautiful purple flowers. It now grows wild, and its roots grow so big and dense that they can block the waterways where they take root. Water lettuce is another invasive species that grows into thick mats and blocks sunlight from plants below it, making it harder for those plants to survive.

PRETTY, BUT INVASIVE!   CREDIT: LIZ WEST (CC BY 2.0)

invasive species: a species that is not native to an ecosystem and that is harmful to it in some way.

climate: the average weather patterns in an area during a long period of time.

climate change: changes to the average weather patterns in an area during a long period of time.

WORDS TO KNOW

Plants are a crucial part of a lake's ecosystem. That's why scientists pay close attention when they notice a plant species that's no longer thriving. That could mean trouble—climate trouble! We'll learn how climate change can affect lakes and ponds in the next chapter.

? CONSIDER AND DISCUSS

It's time to consider and discuss: What type of plants are more important in a lake—small plants that you need a microscope to see or big, leafy plants?

WHAT'S FOR LUNCH?

Lakes and ponds provide an ideal environment for watercress, a leafy green vegetable prized for its strong flavor and rich nutrients. While watercress can often be found growing near lakes and ponds, it's safer to eat watercress that is grown specifically for people to eat. Let's make some wild rice and watercress salad!

Caution: You should never eat plants that you find in the wild.

1 Cook the wild rice according to the package directions. After it's cooked, spread it on a baking sheet to cool.

2 Peel the oranges, making sure to remove as much of the white pith as possible. Segment the oranges, then cut each segment in half. Wash the watercress and shake out any excess water.

3 Plate your salad! Put a small pile of watercress on the plate, then top with wild rice, oranges, and pomegranate seeds. Add dressing to taste.

TRY THIS! Is there an ingredient in this activity that you are allergic to, that is difficult to find locally, or that you simply do not like? Research some alternatives that live in or around lakes and experiment with the recipe. Do you think you could make a version of this salad using food from only your own state?

SUPPLIES

✳ science journal and pencil

PLANT FACTS

Plants that grow in lakes and ponds sometimes adapt to their environments in fun ways! Do some research at the library or on the internet for each plant on the chart. Name the zone it lives in and find a fun fact to share with your friends and classmates.

Caution: Ask an adult for permission to use the internet.

Plant	Zone	Fun Fact
Sphagnum moss		
Reed		
Tussock sedge		
Water lily		
Mermaid weed		
Phytoplankton		

PROJECT!

OBSERVING VASCULAR PLANTS

Some plants have interesting systems for moving nutrients around. For example, vascular plants use tubes called xylem to bring water and nutrients from the roots to the rest of the plant. Phloem are structures that bring sugar made during photosynthesis to different parts of the plant. Let's observe the xylem and phloem of celery stalks.

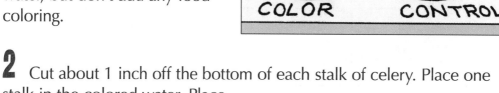

COLOR   CONTROL

1 Fill a cup halfway with water. Add a few drops of food coloring to the water. Remember, green might be more difficult to see! Fill a second cup halfway with water, but don't add any food coloring.

2 Cut about 1 inch off the bottom of each stalk of celery. Place one stalk in the colored water. Place the second stalk of celery into the clear water. This is your control celery.

3 Place each cup on a piece of paper in a sunny spot. Label the papers for the control celery and the colored water celery.

WORDS TO KNOW

vascular: relating to blood vessels in animals and the system that conducts water, sap, and nutrients in plants.

xylem: the tubes in vascular plants through which nutrients travel.

phloem: the structures within plants that bring sugar made during photosynthesis to different parts of the plant.

4 Observe the celery during the course of one hour, several hours, and an entire day. What happens to the celery in a cup with colored water? The one in uncolored water?

THINK ABOUT IT! Why do you think the celery looks the way it did after a couple days? How does this demonstrate a vascular plant? Look inside the celery stalk. Can you see the xylem?

TRY THIS! Repeat the experiment, but this time, place the cups with celery in a spot that does not receive any sunlight. How is the result different? Why?

WORKING WITH PLANTS

If you love plants, you might want to think about becoming a botanist. Botany is a biology science that studies plant life. Botanists study more than 400,000 species of plants, more than 390,000 of which are vascular plants. The rest are bryophytes, or plants that don't have vascular systems. Botany grew out of herbalism, which is using plants as medicine.

WORDS TO KNOW

botany: the study of plants.

biology: the study of life and of living organisms.

PROJECT!

LETTER TO AN IMPRESSIONIST

SUPPLIES

✳ science journal and pencil

Lakes and ponds have inspired centuries of artists and writers. One such artist was French impressionist Claude Monet (1840–1926). He painted about 250 paintings late in his life that depicted water lilies in a pond in his garden.

WATER LILIES, 1916

1 Think about some of the characteristics of Monet's water lilies.

- In what layer or zone of the pond do water lilies grow?

- What type of plant is a water lily?

- What parts of the plant are above water?

- Where are the plant's roots located?

2 Write a letter to Monet in your science journal. Do some research and share some important facts about the water lilies Monet loved so much! Include at least five facts about water lilies and/or the ponds they thrive in.

TRY THIS! Can you find other artists who used water plants as inspiration? How are their paintings different from Monet's?

  You can take a virtual tour of a Water Lilies painting at the Musee de L'Orangerie. How does the painting change as you get closer to it?

KEYWORD PROMPTS

water lilies interactive 🔍

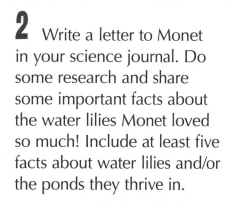

PROJECT!

MOSS ART

You can find different types of moss around lakes and ponds. Moss even grows on the sides of brick or cement. Some people use moss as paint for green art projects. Make your own natural art!

Caution: Ask an adult to help with the blender and for permission to use the paint.

SUPPLIES

* moss (about 2 large clumps)
* 2 cups buttermilk or plain yogurt
* 2 cups water
* ½ teaspoon sugar
* blender
* corn syrup (optional)
* plastic container
* paintbrush
* stencils (optional)

1 Wash the moss to remove as much dirt as possible from it. Place moss, buttermilk or yogurt, water, and sugar in a blender. Blend until just smooth. Ask an adult for help. If you'd like a thicker consistency, add corn syrup. Put the mixture into the plastic container.

2 Head outdoors and find a place to paint. Brick or concrete walls work especially well. Make sure you have permission to paint on them!

3 Paint! Use stencils or paint freehand. Return every week or so to see your artwork develop. You can spray the art with water to encourage growth. You can also repaint as needed to enliven your artwork.

TRY THIS! Can you make characters and scenes with your moss paint? Can you invent a comic strip using this type of drawing?

59

CHAPTER 5

CHANGING LAKES AND PONDS

A lake or pond in summer, when it's full of fish, birds, and swimming people, is very different from the same lake in winter. Imagine taking a swim in Lake Superior in January!

Lakes and ponds change from season to season and also from year to year. As the world's climate changes, waterways are some of the most affected ecosystems. Let's take a look at the difference between changing seasons and a changing climate.

? INVESTIGATE!

How do lakes and ponds change through the four seasons? How is this different from change that happens because of climate change?

CHANGING SEASONS

In Chapter 1, we learned about the three layers of temperature in many lakes. The top layer, or the epilimnion, is the warmest because it's exposed to the most sunlight. The middle, the metalimnion, is cooler. The bottom, the hypolimnion, is coldest.

lake mixing: what happens when the temperature layers in a lake mix due to changing densities.

inverse stratification: when the order of layers are reversed in a lake and cold water rises to the surface while warm water falls lower.

WORDS TO KNOW

SEASONAL HEAT LAYERS

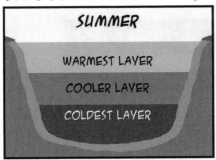

SUMMER
WARMEST LAYER
COOLER LAYER
COLDEST LAYER

SPRING/FALL
LAYERS MIX

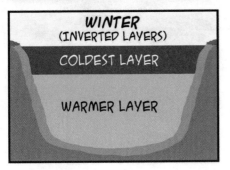

WINTER
(INVERTED LAYERS)
COLDEST LAYER
WARMER LAYER

However, in the spring and the fall, when temperatures are rising or falling, lake mixing occurs. Water becomes denser the colder it gets, until it hits 39 degrees Fahrenheit (3.9 degrees Celsius). In the winter, when water is below 39 degrees, it becomes less dense again.

That means in the summer, the epilimnion is the least dense, because it's the warmest. That's why the top, middle, and lower layers of a lake don't mix.

DID YOU KNOW?

In the winter, inverse stratification occurs. The colder layers are on top of the warmer layers, because the top layer is most exposed to freezing air.

WORDS TO KNOW

mineral: a naturally occurring solid found in rocks and in the ground. Rocks are made of minerals. Gold and diamonds are precious minerals.

WORDS TO KNOW

But in the fall, when the epilimnion starts to cool off, its density is closer to the metalimnion. The layers start to mix! This distributes oxygen and nutrients throughout the water.

Lakes and ponds change day to day and season to season, but some of that normal change is being disrupted by human use, industry, and climate change. Let's explore the factors that are contributing to change in these bodies of water.

CLIMATE CHANGE

Because lakes and ponds are relatively small, they're very responsive to changes in climate. It takes much longer to see a change in an ocean than it does in a lake. Scientists can use data gathered from lakes and ponds to make observations about climate change.

CANADA'S SPOTTED LAKE

Seasons affect some lakes more than others. Spotted Lake in British Columbia, Canada, is filled with rich deposits of silver, titanium, and minerals. In the summer, most of the water evaporates from the shallow lake, leaving behind small pools of concentrated minerals. Those pools look like polka dots of all different colors! People can walk between them and observe the different pools.

CREDIT: JUSTIN RAYCRAFT (CC BY 2.0)

One of the biggest indicators of climate change is the changing water temperature in lakes. Scientists find valuable information by measuring temperatures in the epilimnion, or the top layer, of lakes around the globe. In general, the temperatures are warming. Another indicator is the timing of when lakes freeze, how long they stay frozen, and when they thaw. As global temperatures rise, freezes last for shorter and shorter periods of time.

Scientists are keeping their eyes on other affects of global warming. This includes thawing of glaciers and permafrost, which is a layer of soil that stays frozen all year long in some regions.

Scientists predict climate change will reduce the number of fish and waterfowl in lakes, which will increase mosquito populations and the diseases they spread, such as malaria. They also think that climate change will create more bacteria and more abnormal algal blooms in lakes. This affects the entire balance of ecosystems. It's why conservation is so important!

global warming: the gradual warming of the planet, causing climate change.

permafrost: a layer of soil in cold regions that stays frozen year-round.

conservation: managing and protecting natural resources.

WORDS TO KNOW

WHICH IS THE SCARIEST LAKE TO VISIT ON HALLOWEEN?

Lake Eerie!

THE MYSTERY OF PALAU JELLYFISH LAKE

Palau is a country of more than 500 tiny islands in Oceania, in the western Pacific Ocean. It's full of natural beauty, but the most unique of its features has long been Palau Jellyfish Lake. The lake, full of 20 million golden jellyfish that are so harmless people scuba dive and swim with them, is a natural wonder. Every day, the jellyfish leave one side of the lake and swim to the other, for no explainable reason. But now, the jellyfish have mostly disappeared. Why? Scientists researched the lake and discovered that the disappearing jellyfish had to do with the changing climate. A warming trend, combined with a long and severe drought, lowered the water level in the lake and increased the salinity. The jellyfish can't survive in those conditions. For now, the lake is closed to tourism in the hopes of restoring the jellyfish population.

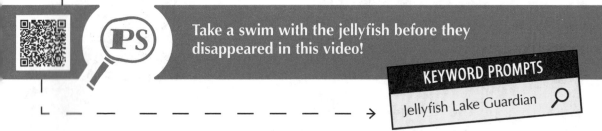

(PS) Take a swim with the jellyfish before they disappeared in this video!

KEYWORD PROMPTS

Jellyfish Lake Guardian 🔍

A CHANGING WATER SUPPLY

When you walk into the grocery store and see an entire aisle full of bottle after bottle of water, it's easy to think that humans have as much water as they could possibly need. After all, most people you know can probably turn on the tap and get water from any sink or water fountain.

WORDS TO KNOW

drought: a long period of little or no rain.

However, that's true only in some areas of the globe. Many people in undeveloped countries don't have access to clean water. As populations grow and the climates change, fresh water is in shorter and shorter supply in many places.

For example, the Ganges Basin in India, which provides millions of people with the water they need, is shrinking by nearly 6 centimeters a year. This may not sound like a lot, but during many years, this will mean less and less water for the people who live there.

Mexico City, the most populous city in the world, draws much of its water from aquifers under the city. But because the aquifers are being emptied faster than they can fill, the city is actually sinking!

DID YOU KNOW?

In some areas, Mexico City is sinking nearly 9 inches a year.

Because of rising global temperatures, water is evaporating into the atmosphere more quickly. This creates periods of very intense rain with flooding and even mudslides, followed by periods of drought. These floods and mudslides are dangerous. In 2017 in Houston, Texas, Hurricane Harvey dumped so much rain that floods forced more than 10,000 people from their homes.

CRATER LAKE

Crater Lake in Oregon is a natural marvel. The lake formed in the crater of a volcano and is the deepest lake in the United States. It has no water source other than rainfall and is known for the purity and clearness of its waters. But because the Crater Lake is on the top of a mountain, it's often invisible! Clouds get trapped inside the crater, blocking the view. They hover over the lake until they rain down water, filling the lake.

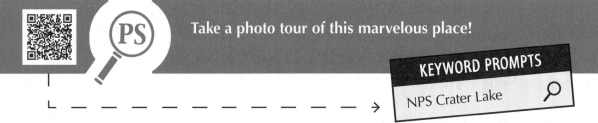

Take a photo tour of this marvelous place!

KEYWORD PROMPTS

NPS Crater Lake

Droughts, such as the one California suffered from 2011 to 2016, impact everything from our ability to grow food to the health of our families and pets. When the drought ended, so much rain fell so quickly that it flooded neighborhoods, stressed dams, and washed out roads, resulting in mudslides that destroyed homes.

As we can see, lakes and ponds play a huge role in keeping Earth's ecosystems in balance, and can also serve as warnings to scientists when the environment is getting more imbalanced. That's why it's important to work at practicing conservation whenever possible! We'll look at how we can help keep the earth healthy in the next chapter.

CONSIDER AND DISCUSS

It's time to consider and discuss: How do lakes and ponds change through the four seasons? How is this different from change that happens because of climate change?

PROJECT!

SIMULATING THE DEATH OF A LAKE

As time passes—whether it is weeks or hundreds of thousands of years—lakes and ponds can "die." The basin that makes up the lake or pond can get completely filled with sediment so water has nowhere to collect. Let's see what this looks like.

1 Place a small amount of your natural sediment in the pan. Fill the pan with water about halfway.

2 Add more of the sediment to the pan. As you add sediment, write your observations in your science journal about what is happening to your small lake.

3 Continue adding more and more sediment until most of the water in your lake has been absorbed by the natural materials. Record your observations.

DID YOU KNOW?

When a lake totally evaporates, it leaves a dry lakebed behind. These areas are rich in minerals and salts, and are important sources of nutrition for animals. Dry lakebeds are also rich in artifacts, and archaeologists often dig in dry lakebeds to find clues to human history.

THINK ABOUT IT!

As you added more and more dirt, sticks, rocks, leaves, and other natural material to your pond, what happened to the water? How does this show the way a pond or lake can change over time?

WORDS TO KNOW

artifact: an object made by people in the past, including tools, pottery, and jewelry.

archaeologist: a person who studies ancient people through the objects they left behind.

67

PROJECT!

FLOATING ICE, HIBERNATING POND LIFE

When you put ice cubes into a glass of water, what happens to the ice? Does it sink to the bottom of the glass? Or does it bob up to the top? Ice on lakes and ponds behaves the same way. Use your supplies to design a model of a lake in winter.

SUPPLIES

* large clear bowl
* water
* pond life figurines such as turtles and frogs
* dirt and/or gravel or stones
* ice cubes

1 Fill the large bowl about halfway to two-thirds full of water.

2 Next, place animals that you believe are hibernators in the water into the bowl. Watch them sink to the bottom.

3 Next, add ice cubes to the bowl. Add enough ice so that when the cubes are spread out they form a layer of ice that completely covers the surface of the water.

4 If you have animal figurines that you believe live on or near lakes and ponds during the winter, place those animal figurines where they would usually live in the winter.

THINK ABOUT IT! Why do you think ice floats on top of the water instead of sinking to the bottom? As the air in winter gets colder, what happens to the water in the lake or pond? How can you represent that with your supplies? Regardless of which animal figurines you used for this activity, rate where the following lake and pond dwellers would likely spend their winters: Turtle, frog, duck, goose, fish, and dragonfly nymphs.

CHAPTER 6

PRACTICING CONSERVATION!

We learned in the last chapter about some of the
ways lakes and ponds are changing because of
a changing climate. But how did it start?

The Industrial Revolution began in the eighteenth century when
clever inventors thought of new machines and ways to produce
all kinds of different
goods in factories. Since
then humans have been
building more, making
more, and consuming more.

? INVESTIGATE!

What are ways we can all
work together to help preserve
our earth's natural resources?

LAKES AND PONDS!

These machines run by burning fossil fuels, which produces carbon dioxide. Lots and lots of carbon dioxide. As levels of carbon dioxide in the atmosphere have increased, the atmosphere has warmed.

In the nineteenth century, people didn't know much about pollution. They dumped harmful chemicals in water or buried them in the ground. As populations have grown and technology has developed, more and more environmental stressors have been placed on lakes. Waterways are suffering.

Though many countries have designed ways to decrease future pollution and are working to reverse the effects of past pollution, the task is enormous. For example, the Great Lakes have high levels of mercury, which has affected the fish population. Many other kinds of pollution in these lakes make them unsafe for people and wildlife alike. Lake Erie, in particular, is full of tiny particles of plastic, which can kill birds and fish.

PLASTIC POLLUTION FLOATING ON A LAKE

In other parts of the world too, lake pollution is an active problem. In January 2018, a massive fire broke out on a lake in India when the chemicals and construction waste in it caught fire. It took 5,000 soldiers to get the blaze under control.

HOW CAN YOU HELP?

Now it's time to talk about the actions you can take every day to help heal our earth and its lakes and ponds!

Everyone needs to pitch in to help conserve our lakes and ponds, but the work kids do is especially important. When you make big changes toward conserving lakes and ponds, precious water reserves can be protected far into the future.

DID YOU KNOW?

In 1800, fewer than 1 billion people lived on the planet. In 2017, there are more than 7 billion of us! Scientists predict that we'll add another billion people to that number in the next 20 years. That's a lot of people who need food and fresh water.

ALGAL BLOOM

Nutrients are necessary to plants and animals—but there can be too much of a good thing! Farms use a lot of fertilizer in their fields, and when it rains, some of the nutrients from that fertilizer can run off into nearby lakes and ponds. When a lake or pond has too many nutrients, it can result in an overgrowth of plants, especially algae. This can cause an abnormal algal bloom. If the body of water gets totally overtaken with algae, it throws off the balance of the ecosystem in a lake or pond and can be harmful to other species.

Let's explore different ways you can conserve the water and habitats of lakes and ponds.

CONSERVATION HABITS

As we have learned, some of the fresh water we use every day comes from lakes and ponds. We need to conserve and protect this water. One way is to use less water during the day-to-day activities of life. For example, you can turn off the water while you brush your teeth.

CREATIVE WATER CONSERVATION

Here are some creative ways to conserve water!

* Use dirty fish tank water to water houseplants. You'll save some water, plus the plants will benefit from the nutrients in the dirty fish bowl water.

* Use sprinklers wisely. If you want to cool off in a sprinkler on a summer day, place the sprinkler in an area that will also be watering some plants. Also invite friends over so more people are benefitting from the use of the sprinkler!

* Fill the sink with a couple inches of soapy water to wash dishes instead of washing them under running water.

* Talk to your family about using a rain barrel for watering the lawn and outdoor plants instead of tap water.

* Make sure dishwashers and washing machines are full so the wash cycle is cleaning the maximum number of items.

You can even use less water in the shower by using water only at the beginning and end of a shower. First, use water to get wet, then turn water off while you lather, and turn water back on to rinse.

Conservation isn't just about using less water in your local area, though. It is also about protecting the habitats around lakes and ponds so that the wildlife that support these waterways thrive. This includes never littering. Pick up trash whenever you visit a lake or pond.

One example of a pond that needs to be conserved is Walden Pond in Concord, Massachusetts. Henry David Thoreau (1817–1862) made its amazingly clear water famous with his writings. Since the time of Thoreau, however, high numbers of visitors to the pond have added nutrients to the water with their activities and caused a shift in the balance of the pond's ecosystem. This has made the water more murky.

CREDIT: JOHN PHELAN (CC BY 3.0)

CLIMATE CHANGE KIDS

The effects of climate change are also posing a threat to lakes and ponds. You can help prevent further changes to the earth's climate in many ways!

* Conserve energy by unplugging and turning things off and by using less air conditioning and heating.

DID YOU KNOW?

Why is water so important to us? Human bodies are made up of 60 percent water. Our bones are 31 percent water!

* Plant your own fruits and vegetables. Not only will the plants help reduce the amount of carbon dioxide in the air, but you won't have to purchase as much food that has been shipped to you on big trucks.

* Share carpool rides with friends.

* Spread the message by sharing your conservation ideas with your friends.

Lakes and ponds are incredibly important to the plants, animals, and humans who live, work, and play around waterways. They are also crucial to the delicate environmental balance that keeps our planet healthy and thriving for everyone!

CONSIDER AND DISCUSS

It's time to consider and discuss: What are ways we can all work together to help preserve our earth's natural resources?

PROJECT!

POND PROTECTORS

Litter and pollution have negative effects on lakes and ponds and the plants and animals that live in and around them. Kids have the power to help the ecosystems of lakes and ponds, as well as other vital habitats in the environment.

SUPPLIES

* latex or rubber gloves
* trash bags
* recycling bags
* science journal and pencil

Caution: As you clean up your environment, make sure to practice safety. Never pick up broken glass, syringes, or anything sharp or dangerous. Alert an adult if you encounter anything dangerous.

1 Decide where you will be a pond protector! You don't even have to go to a lake or pond. Litter that goes down storm drains can make its way to lakes and ponds or other waterways.

2 When you see litter, put on your gloves and pick it up. Sort litter into trash and recyclables. Find out whether your community has single-stream recycling—meaning all paper, cans, plastic, and glass can be recycled together—or whether you need to separate your recyclables.

THINK ABOUT IT! After your cleanup session, reflect in your science journal about the kinds of things you found. How do you think they got there? What would have happened if the litter had made its way into a lake or pond? How could it have harmed the ecosystem? How can you help prevent litter and pollution in your neighborhood?

MOSQUITO TRAP

Mosquitoes are a fact of life in many parts of the United States, either in the summer or year-round. Make a mosquito trap to keep these blood-suckers at bay!

Caution: Ask an adult to help you cut the empty bottle.

1 With an adult's help, cut off the top third of the empty bottle. Put the brown sugar in the bottom of the bottle.

2 Add warm water and stir to mix. Add yeast and stir again.

3 Place the top of the bottle inside the bottom so the opening is facing down. The bottle opening should be at least an inch away from the brown sugar mixture.

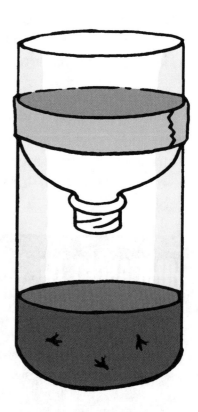

4 Tape the edge of the bottle and bottle spout to prevent any gaps and help keep the spout in place.

5 Place outside and see if you catch any mosquitoes!

ALL ABOUT MOSQUITOES

You've probably had an itchy, red mosquito bite before—and you know they're no fun at all. But did you know that there are more than 175 kinds of mosquitoes in America? The temperature has a lot to do with how many mosquitoes there are near you. Mosquitoes prefer temperatures above 80 degrees, and hibernate when the temperature is under 50. The state with the least variety of mosquitos is West Virginia, with only 26 types. Texas has 85 kinds and Florida has 80.

THINK ABOUT IT!

Humans—and other animals that mosquitoes like to bite—attract mosquitoes with the carbon dioxide that we breathe out. It's a mosquito's clue that a meal is nearby! They follow the carbon dioxide until they find the animal to feed off. In our experiment, carbon dioxide is produced as the yeast feeds on the sugar water and multiplies. Mosquitoes follow that trail of carbon dioxide to the bottom of the bottle. Because of the funnel shape, they can't get out.

DID YOU KNOW?

The longest place name in the United States is Lake Chargoggagoggmanchauggagoggchaubunagungamaugg in Webster, Massachusetts. In Nipmuck, a Native American language, the name means, "fishing place at the boundaries—neutral meeting grounds," or "lake divided by islands."

MISSION: WATER CONSERVATION

The water cycle shows us that the total amount of water on Earth does not change and it is never used up. Our water just moves from one place to another in a constant cycle. But within the water cycle, water can be polluted and it can be scarce in many areas. The earth's reserves of clean fresh water are not unlimited. For example, in 2017 and 2018, the city of Cape Town, South Africa, was at risk of running out of fresh water after a long drought. The city implemented strict water restrictions and tracked what was called Day Zero, when the city would run out of water. Thankfully, conservation cut water consumption in half and rain brought relief before February's Day Zero. Cape Town's water supply is still low, but Day Zero has been postponed, at least for now. Let's estimate how much water you use in a typical day.

1 In your science journal, write down all the ways you and your family use water. Think of everything, from food (what you drink and how you use water in cooking) to hygiene (washing your hands, flushing the toilet, taking showers) to lifestyle (filling a swimming pool, washing the car, watering the lawn).

WHY WE NEED TO CONSERVE WATER

When water comes out of the faucet every time you turn it on, it's hard to understand that we need to conserve this precious resource. Remember—even though you might have plenty of water to drink, to wash with, and to water your plants, not everybody has that much water. Much of the world struggles to find clean water, including 63 million Americans. In places such as Flint, Michigan, the water coming out of the pipes is polluted and has made people sick.

PROJECT!

2 Now play a matching game! Using two lists below, match the activity to the number of gallons of water used.

* Flushing the toilet
* Taking a shower
* Washing dishes
* Brushing teeth
* Drinking water
* Watering the garden
* Washing clothing

* 1 gallon
* ½ gallon
* 15–30 gallons
* 30 gallons
* 180 gallons
* 4–7 gallons
* 9–20 gallons

3 Check your answers in the resources section. How many did you get correct? Look at your original list of uses for water in your everyday life. Does your list have anything that was not in the matching list? Can you estimate how much water those activities might take? Add up how many gallons of water you use in a day. What's your total?

TRY THIS! Take a hard look at that list. Can you use less water in any way? List some ways you and your family might try to conserve fresh water and have a family discussion about making some of those changes.

PROJECT!

MAKE A WATER METER

SUPPLIES

✳ cardboard
✳ paper plate
✳ 2 brad fasteners
✳ scissors
✳ ruler
✳ marker

Every home that is connected to a town water service has a water meter. The water meter keeps track of how much water is used by a house or building. The town water company reads the meter to charge the owner of the building or home for the water it has used. In this activity, we will make a homemade water meter to demonstrate how to read a water meter.

1 Cut one piece of cardboard about 2 inches shorter than the radius of the paper plate—the radius is the point in the middle of the plate to the edge of the plate. This will be the sweeper: think of it like the minute hand on a clock!

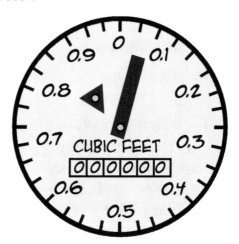

2 Cut another piece of cardboard in a triangle shape that will just fit over the head of a brad fastener.

3 Draw the numbers on the edges of the paper plate to indicate how much water is used. See the diagram for a common way water meters are numbered.

WORDS TO KNOW

radius: the distance from the center of a circle to any point on the circle.

MEASURING WATER

Many water meters show how many cubic feet of water are used. This number is then calculated into the number of gallons of water used. One cubic foot of water equals 7.48 gallons of water.

4 Punch the brad fastener through the bottom of the sweeper. Then, punch it through the center of the paper plate.

5 Using the other brad fastener, attach the cardboard triangle to the paper plate as it is in the picture.

6 Alone or with a partner, simulate how the water meter would move during an average shower. Hint: The average shower lasts around eight minutes and uses 20 gallons of water. A cubic foot of water is 7.48 gallons of water. So, a water meter would go through just under three revolutions during an average shower!

TRY THIS! The little triangle on a water meter helps detect water leaks. To check your home for a leak, make sure all the water is turned off in the house and in the yard. Find the water meter (it's usually in a little metal box near the street). If the triangle is moving even with all the water turned off, there is a water leak somewhere!

UNDERSTANDING HABITAT LOSS

All living things must have their basic needs met in order to survive. What are your basic needs? When lake creatures' needs are easily met, they flourish and are able to reproduce. As the number of a species grows, sometimes their habitat can't support as many new creatures. Or, when habitats are destroyed through human activity such as pollution, the habitat might no longer meet the needs of all members of a species. Let's play a game of musical chairs to see this. In this game, people will represent members of a made-up lake species.

1 Place the 10 chairs in two rows of five, with the backs of the chairs facing each other. Six people representing the lake species start the game. Play musical chairs as you normally would. What happens when the music stops?

2 Add a new generation! Add three people to the original six, but keep the same amount of resources or chairs. Play musical chairs again. What happens?

3 Keep adding new generations, but with each new generation, take away a chair. What happens?

THINK ABOUT IT! What happened as new generations were added to the population? How can we use that to think about habitat loss?

A

absorb: to soak up.

adapt: to make changes to better survive in an environment.

algae: a plant-like organism that lives in water and grows by converting energy from the sun into food.

algal bloom: abnormal growth of algae in a body of water.

amphibian: a cold-blooded animal with moist skin that is born in water but lives on land. Frogs, toads, newts, efts, and salamanders are amphibians.

aquaculture: the farming of fish and other organisms that live in the water.

aquatic: living or growing in water.

aquifer: an underground layer of rock that has space in it that holds water.

archaeologist: a person who studies ancient people through the objects they left behind.

artifact: an object made by people in the past, including tools, pottery, and jewelry.

asteroid: a small, rocky object that orbits the sun.

astrobiologist: a scientist who studies life in space.

atmosphere: a blanket of gases around the earth.

B

bacteria: microorganisms that live in animals, plants, soil, and water. Some bacteria are helpful and some are harmful.

basin: a hollow in the land into which water flows, forming a waterway.

biology: the study of life and of living organisms.

botany: the study of plants.

brackish: water that contains both salt water and fresh water.

buoyancy: the ability to float.

C

carbon dioxide: a colorless, odorless gas. It forms when animals breathe and when plants and other living matter die and rot.

celestial body: a star, planet, moon, or other object in space.

climate: the average weather patterns in an area during a long period of time.

climate change: changes to the average weather patterns in an area during a long period of time.

cold-blooded: animals that have a body temperature that varies with the surrounding temperature, such as fish and snakes.

condensation: the process of a gas cooling down and changing into a liquid.

conservation: managing and protecting natural resources.

crater: a large, bowl-shaped hole in the ground caused by an impact.

crater lake: a lake formed by a collapsed volcano.

crops: plants grown for food and other uses.

crustacean: a type of animal, such as a crab or lobster, that lives mainly in water. It has several pairs of legs and its body is made up of sections covered in a hard outer shell.

cyanobacteria: a type of aquatic bacteria that produces oxygen through photosynthesis.

D

dam: a natural or man-made barrier to flowing water.

decomposer: an organism that breaks down dead matter and provides nutrients to other organisms and to the soil and air.

density: a measure of how closely packed items are.

depression: a hole or low spot in the land.

drought: a long period of little or no rain.

E

economy: the wealth and resources of an area or country.

ecosystem: a community of living and nonliving things and their environment. Living things are plants, animals, and insects. Nonliving things are soil, rocks, and water.

environmental stressor: pollutants in the atmosphere and water.

environment: a natural area with animals, plants, rocks, soil, and water.

epilimnion: the top layer of lake water.

erode: to gradually wear away.

estimate: to make a close guess.

evaporation: the process of a liquid heating up and becoming a gas.

evolve: to gradually develop through time.

extraterrestrial lake: a lake formed in the crater left by the impact of an asteroid or meteorite.

F

fisheries: places where fish are caught or raised as a business.

flooding: when water covers an area that is usually dry.

food chain: a community of plants and animals, where each is eaten by another higher up in the chain.

food web: a network of connected food chains that shows the complex set of feeding relationships between plants and animals.

fossil fuels: a source of energy that comes from plants and animals that lived millions of years ago. These include coal, oil, and natural gas.

fungi: organisms without leaves or flowers that grow on other plants or decaying material. Singular is fungus.

G

gills: filter-like structures that let an organism get oxygen out of the water to breathe.

glacial lake: a lake formed by the movement of glaciers.

glaciation: the process of glaciers carving out depressions in the land, which later became lakes.

glacier: a huge mass of ice and snow.

global warming: the gradual warming of the planet, causing climate change.

goods: items that can be bought, sold, or traded.

groundwater: water held underground in the soil or in cracks and crevices in rocks.

H

habitat: the natural area where a plant or animal lives.

hibernate: to spend a period of time in an inactive state in order to survive harsh conditions.

hydrocarbon: a chemical compound that contains hydrogen and carbon. Oil and natural gas are hydrocarbons.

hydroelectric power: electricity created by harnessing the energy of moving water.

hypolimnion: the deepest layer of lake water.

I

ice age: a period of time when ice covers a large part of the earth.

Industrial Revolution: a period of time beginning in the late 1700s when people started using machines to make things in large factories.

industry: a business that provides a product or service.

interconnectivity: the state of being connected together.

Inuit: the native people who live in northern Canada, parts of Greenland, and Alaska.

invasive species: a species that is not native to an ecosystem and that is harmful to the ecosystem in some way.

inverse stratification: when the order of layers are reversed in a lake and cold water rises to the surface while warm water falls lower.

invertebrate: an animal without a backbone.

irrigation: the process of delivering water to plants or fields where crops are planted.

L

lake mixing: what happens when the temperature layers in a lake mix due to changing densities.

larva: an organism at the beginning stage of development. Plural is larvae.

life cycle: the growth and changes an organism goes through from birth to death.

limnetic zone: the top layer of water in a lake or pond farther from the shoreline where only algae and other phytoplankton grow.

limnologist: a person who studies inland waterways.

littoral zone: the shallow area of a lake near the shoreline where sunlight can reach the bottom.

M

mammal: a type of animal, such as a human, dog, or cat. Mammals are born live, feed milk to their young, and usually have hair or fur covering most of their skin.

metalimnion: the middle layer of lake water.

metamorphosis: an animal's complete change in physical form as it develops into an adult.

meteorite: a meteor, which is a small piece of rock from space that hits the earth's surface.

microclimate: the climate of a very small area.

microscopic: something so small it can be seen only with a microscope.

mineral: a naturally occurring solid found in rocks and in the ground. Rocks are made of minerals. Gold and diamonds are precious minerals.

mining: taking minerals from the ground, such as silver or iron ore.

mollusk: an animal with a soft body protected by a shell, such as a clam or snail.

mudslide: a moving mass of soil and other materials.

N

natural resource: something found in nature that is useful to humans, such as water to drink, trees to burn and build with, and fish to eat.

nutrients: substances in food and soil that living things need to live and grow.

O

organic lake: a lake formed by animals or when clumps of vegetation or mud stops the flow of water.

organism: a living thing, such as an animal or a plant.

outlet: a river or stream connected to a lake or other body of water that allows water to flow out.

overfishing: when so many fish are caught each year that populations decline.

oxygenate: to supply with oxygen.

P

permafrost: a layer of soil in cold regions that stays frozen year-round.

phloem: the structures within plants that bring sugar made during photosynthesis to different parts of the plant.

photosynthesis: the process plants use to turn sunlight, carbon dioxide, and water into food.

phytoplankton: tiny, free-floating plants that live in both fresh water and salt water.

pollution: harmful materials that damage the air, water, and soil. These include chemicals and factory waste.

populous: heavily populated by people.

precipitation: the falling to the earth of rain, snow, or any form of water.

predator: an animal that hunts other animals for food.

prey: an animal that is killed by another for food.

profundal zone: the deepest waters of a lake where no sunlight reaches.

purification: the process of making fresh water safe for humans to drink.

R

radius: the distance from the center of a circle to any point on the circle.

reptile: a cold-blooded animal such as a snake, lizard, alligator, or turtle, that has a spine, lays eggs, has scales or horny places, and breathes air.

reservoir: a man-made or natural lake used to store water for drinking and other uses.

restriction: a limit on something.

S

saline: describes lakes and ponds that contain salt.

scarcity: too little of something.

scavenge: to feed on animals that are already dead.

sediment: bits of rock, sand, or dirt that have been carried to a place by water, wind, or a glacier.

solar system: the collection of eight planets, moons, and other celestial bodies that orbit the sun.

species: a group of living things that have similar characteristics and can produce offspring.

stalactite: a cave formation that looks like an icicle hanging from the ceiling.

stalagmite: a cave formation that sticks up from the floor, often under a stalactite.

subglacial lake: a freshwater lake underneath a glacier.

surface water: water that collects in lakes, rivers, and oceans on the surface of the earth.

T

technology: the tools, methods, and systems used to solve a problem or do work.

tectonic lake: a lake formed in cracks made by the movement of tectonic plates.

tectonic plates: large sections of the earth's crust that move on top of the hot, melted layer below.

thermal pollution: a form of water pollution in which the temperature of a lake is altered when it is used to cool machinery.

thermal stratification: the separation of a lake into three different zones of temperature.

tourism: the business of people traveling for fun.

turbine: a machine that produces energy from moving liquid or air.

V

vascular: relating to blood vessels in animals and the system that conducts water, sap, and nutrients in plants.

vegetation: all the plant life in a particular area.

vertebrate: an animal with a backbone.

W

warm-blooded: animals that can keep themselves warm with their own body heat, such as humans, birds, and bears.

water cycle: the continuous movement of water from the earth to the clouds and back again.

water vapor: the gas form of water.

Western Hemisphere: the half of the earth that contains North and South America.

winterkill: when plants and fish die in frozen lakes due to reduced oxygen levels.

X

xylem: the tubes in vascular plants through which nutrients travel.

Z

zooplankton: tiny animals that float freely in salt water and fresh water.

METRIC CONVERSIONS

Use this chart to find the metric equivalents to the English measurements in this book. If you need to know a half measurement, divide by two. If you need to know twice the measurement, multiply by two. How do you find a quarter measurement? How do you find three times the measurement?

English	Metric
1 inch	2.5 centimeters
1 foot	30.5 centimeters
1 yard	0.9 meter
1 mile	1.6 kilometers
1 pound	0.5 kilogram
1 teaspoon	5 milliliters
1 tablespoon	15 milliliters
1 cup	237 milliliters

WEBSITES

Clean Water Action: A volunteer organization that works to educate the public about the dangers of polluted water.
CleanWaterAction.org

The Water Project: An organization working to bring clean water to Africa, with a website full of good information on how clean water impacts our health, our planet, and our lives.
TheWaterProject.org

Environmental Protection Agency: The U.S. government organization that works to protect the environment, including preserving our freshwater sources. Read about the Clean Water Act at this website.
EPA.gov

A Brief History of the Clean Water Act: A timeline of the efforts America has taken to keep its lakes and other fresh water clean, starting in 1968.
PBS.org/Now/Science/CleanWater.html

National Geographic: Read all about lakes and ponds around the world, including lakes and ponds throughout history.
NationalGeographic.com

NASA Precipitation Education: Find more information on the water cycle and how we measure rain from NASA.
PMM.NASA.gov/Education

National Park Service: Read about the incredible natural features in America's national parks, from geysers in Yellowstone to the Colorado River running through the Grand Canyon.
NPS.gov

Atlas Obscura: Unusual history, including shipwrecks and other important events that happened in lakes.
AtlasObscura.com

Live Science: Read about scientific topics currently in the news, including climate change.
LiveScience.com

National Agricultural Library: Read about invasive plant species, including the ones that live in and around lakes and ponds.
InvasiveSpeciesInfo.gov

QR CODE GLOSSARY

Page 11: youtube.com/watch?v=m22Lp5NhgCU

Page 14: nps.gov/media/photo/gallery.htm?id= 8C3F542C-1DD8-B71C-0728C0BC176BA864

Page 29: youtube.com/watch?v=jf6TSh3mwfY

Page 47: penguinwatch.org/#

Page 58: musee-orangerie.fr/en/article/water-lilies-virtual-visit

Page 64: theguardian.com/environment/video/2013/ aug/28/swim-jellyfish-lake-palau-video

Page 66: nps.gov/media/photo/gallery.htm?id= F274B442-155D-4519-3E0EF185EDB7DB2F

ESSENTIAL QUESTIONS

Introduction: Why are lakes and ponds important to humans and animals?

Chapter 1: Imagine a day without water. What kinds of activities would you need to give up? What would be different about your day?

Chapter 2: How does human activity affect lakes and ponds?

Chapter 3: What are some ways that humans rely on the animals that live in ponds and lakes?

Chapter 4: What type of plants are more important in a lake—small plants that you need a microscope to see or big, leafy plants?

Chapter 5: How do lakes and ponds change through the four seasons? How is this different from change that happens because of climate change?

Chapter 6: What are ways we can all work together to help preserve our earth's natural resources?

MATCH GAME ANSWERS

Flushing the toilet	4-7 gallons		Brushing teeth	1 gallon
Taking a shower	15-30 gallons		Drinking water	½ gallon
Washing dishes	9-20 gallons		Watering the garden	180 gallons
			Washing clothing	30 gallons